SEAHAWK

CONFESSIONS OF AN
OLD HOCKEY GOALIE

❖ ❖ ❖

BRUCE VALLEY

❖ ❖ ❖

Saugus Public Library
295 Central Street
Saugus, MA 01906

PETER E. RANDALL PUBLISHER LLC
Portsmouth, New Hampshire
2009

© Copyright 2009 by Bruce Valley. All rights reserved.

ISBN10: 1-931807-72-8
ISBN13: 978-1-931807-72-2

Library of Congress Control Number: 2008936907

Published by
Peter E. Randall Publisher LLC
Box 4726
Portsmouth, NH 03802
www.perpublisher.com

Book design: Grace Peirce

Additional copies available from:
www.ryeseahawks.com

Front cover photo: A view six decades into the past through the author's modern goalkeeper helmet and mask. The scene is Rye, New Hampshire's town team hockey rink in late 1948. The Rye Seahawks players, left to right: Bill Jenness, Bill Moulton, and Frank Drake.

To former teammates
Phil Drake, Leighton Remick,
Bill Jenness, and Jack Hayes,
who conceived the Seahawks idea,
brought it to reality, and saw it
through to the end.

To my grandsons,
Jeb and Wilson Milam
and Max and Carson Marr,
who I hope will carry on with this
game when I no longer can.

Contents

WINTER SOLITUDE

Daylight still eludes—the cold so pervasive it reaches through clothes and skin to your bones. A deep silence reigns over the shadowed pond. Stillness everywhere.

No possibility of snow at such temperatures—or of lacing skates unless the job is done quickly.

Taking a first stride as I slip gloves on and reach reflexively for a puck from my pocket, I see before me in the pre-dawn that magical surface of which all hockey players dream—an endless expanse of unbroken, untouched, gleaming black ice.

Alone, I poke amiably at the black disk with my old Northland Pro, then begin a circuit, dodging and weaving to fend off imaginary foes.

The crisp sound of blades cutting ice rasps in the frigid air. The birches seem to quiver at the noise.

An owl stares down from the height of an old oak.

Unimpressed.

—Bruce Valley

Introduction

This book was written for the love of a game. For hockey.

Most would find a certain incongruity between the speed, violence, and apparent brutishness of hockey and the softness, caring, and intimacy of the emotion we call love. My half-century of playing hockey, however, suggests nothing of the kind. There is no incongruity at all.

No other contact sport inspires the enduring loyalty and deep love that hockey does—not football, not rugby, not soccer. And while hockey fans are legend, the true believers are those who have actually played the game.

I will concede that hockey has its violent side—as, of course, does life—and that arming armored men (and today, increasingly, women) with sticks and putting them on razor-sharp blades that propel them into each other at speeds of over fifty miles per hour will cause high emotion and occasional fisticuffs, the latter an activity singularly tolerated, though also penalized, in hockey.

The bumper stickers ("bumpah stickahs," in my native northern New England) attest vividly to hockey's violent nature. I Went To A Fight—and A Hockey Game Broke Out! says one. Or more pointedly, Give Blood: Play Hockey! Hockey's reputation definitely precedes it.

But there is another side to the game, a side seen by those actually taking their shifts on the ice and, perhaps most clearly, by the player behind the mask, the goaltender or goalie—the position I have played for most of my life. Goaltenders often observe the game much as a society matron might watch a ballet—as a delicate interweaving of speed and skill and color in a continuously flowing pattern requiring split-second timing and reaction—a creation of consummate beauty.

The bond among hockey players—and even with their opponents—transcends competition. Only true aficionados understand this. Despite crunching open-ice hits and thunderous checking into end or sideboards that momentarily displace boards and glass, few players are ever badly hurt. Most middle-aged hockey players or ex-players still have usable ankles, knees, and hips, something those who have played football, rugby, soccer, basketball, or even baseball as serious amateurs cannot usually claim.

What is perhaps most telling is that, from childhood peewee leagues to the Stanley Cup finals of the National Hockey League, each game or series, however fierce and unforgiving the play, ends with the opposing teams forming a line at center ice to shake hands and congratulate one another. Players have performed this ritual for more than a century, a tradition that speaks to the very essence of the game.

I grew up in Rye, a small town on the Atlantic seacoast of New Hampshire. Rye was a "hockey town." We ate, slept, talked, and played the game as if it was our very life. Hockey *was* our life. America was going through a time of transition. The Great Depression and World War II lay behind us. Television and other mass media, the national highway system, and prosperity lay ahead. Thus, although jobs were scarce and most people had little money, we shared a sense of contentment and gratitude that the world was again at peace, and a hopeful feeling that things would improve. And they did.

In that suspended state between combat and career, Rye's returning war veterans formed a hockey team—at first informal, then loosely organized, and finally equipped as a team representing the town. The Seahawks played clubs all over northern New England. In their golden era—from 1948 to 1953—the Seahawks were a dominant hockey club, in part because of skilled talent obtained from discontinued teams of fellow veterans in nearby towns. From 1950 to 1952, the Seahawks played for a New Hampshire Class B state championship and a New England Class B championship in the venerable Boston Garden.

By the mid-1950s, much of the Seahawks talent, particularly on offense, had left the team due to career and family obligations or because they had simply grown too old to compete. Looking to add speed and energy, the team brought up four local teenagers to supplement the core of World War II veterans remaining, and other veterans who had joined the team after returning from the Korean conflict.

At the age of fourteen, I became the Seahawks' goaltender, and played that position for the better part of two thrilling yet terrifying seasons (1958–1960), the latter marking the end of the team's play. In 1960, hockey and academic aspiration took me to nearby Phillips Exeter Academy. Later I attended the U.S. Naval Academy at Annapolis. I spent the next two decades in the Navy, where I flew from aircraft carriers, tested experimental aircraft, and took my turn serving in Vietnam. After my naval career, I joined the aerospace industry. I first managed a defense corporation for others, then founded my own.

Hockey has remained my avocation through it all, stretching all the way back to my days with the Seahawks. I have enjoyed playing around the world and around our country—against highly skilled teams and some less skilled, and against those older and much younger. And always, I have returned in winter to my hometown, to Rye, to skate and to play hockey against players I have now known for over half a century, and their sons, and, more recently, their grandsons.

This book has been a living idea for much of that journey.

Rye Seahawk's Rink under construction, winter of 1947–48. Grey Gull Apartments loom in background.

1

BOYHOOD DREAMS OF SNOW AND ICE

Not yesterday I learned to know the love of bare
November days
—Robert Frost

*I*t is at best a dim recollection, formed unclearly in my mind as a goldfish might see foggily out of its bowl—vague and distorted—and with the colors slowly fading as in an old photograph. But here is how I recall the view from the windows of an upper floor looking eastward out of the Grey Gull Apartments—or the White Elephant Apartments, as they were often called because of their lumpy size and brightness—on Myrica Avenue in Rye, New Hampshire. My family lived there after World War II, when the men had finally come home after long years away and the world was beginning to put itself back together.

I was about three years old, which would have made it 1946. My father had mustered out of the Navy and returned to work as a shipfitter at the naval shipyard in nearby Kittery, Maine. Though nothing was ever said openly, a sense of security had returned to our family and our community. The men were back.

From that second-floor vantage point, I could see two small freshwater ponds, which I knew from walks with my mother contained a magical world of turtles, fish, muskrats, ducks, and geese. The ponds sat along Ocean Boulevard, Route 1A. Across the boulevard stood a row of seaside summer homes. Finally, stretching as far as my eye could see and my imagination could conjure, was the great dark blue expanse of the Atlantic Ocean. On certain days I would spend hours mesmerized by the Atlantic—its color, its texture, its moods, its sounds—never guessing that in its siren's song, I was hearing the call to the sea profession I would later follow. But that is another story—a story about blue water; this one is about white or black ice.

New England winters in the 1940s and 1950s were unlike today's relatively mild events. They howled and swirled with snow, sleet, and ice for months on end. It was not uncommon to have at least one heavy storm each winter bringing two or three feet of snow. Many more brought perhaps a foot. Photos of Rye families in those days show the snow reaching up to the first-floor windows of their houses. It took teams of men to shovel the distance from their clusters of homes to the roads. The roads themselves could be cleared only by huge V-plows.

Apart from all the shoveling, not much happened outdoors in Rye in those harsh winters following the war. In a small rural town of some fifteen hundred souls, the one thing a small boy lacked watching from his second-floor aerie was action to fill the landscape. Except for the occasional automobile or snowplow, or a single figure struggling along the boulevard or beach, my upstairs view of the town in winter never varied. It was a virtual still life. This scarcity of activity owed something to a lack of possessions—difficult to imagine amid today's overabundance and frenetic schedules. During the early 1940s, all industrial production served the war effort. Automobiles and many other commodities were not produced for several years. Consumables such as tires, gasoline, and oil remained in very short supply after the war, and were subject to rationing. In the immediate postwar environment, neither jobs nor goods were available in ample supply. As a result, people were cautious with their habits and with their spending.

But then one afternoon this static tableau suddenly came to life. Walking to the window to survey my realm, I discovered below, and to my great delight, a little boy's ultimate gift. Action! Out on the frozen pond a group of men skated vigorously to and fro. They held sticks and batted at some object on the ice. Then they batted at each other. Some were falling down—or being knocked down! Even through the storm windows, I heard laughter, shouting, curses. I was mesmerized.

The game was still going on when my father arrived home from the shipyard. He explained that the men were enjoying a game called "hockey," or "shinny" in the more casual form it was being played on the pond. The players, he said, were all war veterans who had come home to Rye from years away. Many had suffered terrible experiences in combat. With jobs so scarce, he thought getting together to skate, exercise, and play hockey with childhood friends would probably help them adjust to being home again.

The informal hockey games became my primary entertainment in those pre-TV days. I almost never missed one. Gradually I came to recognize a few names, those of players my parents knew. Their skill amazed me. How fast they skated, how deftly they stick handled. But even as a little boy, I was most impressed by how much hitting went on in those friendly matches, and no one seemed to get hurt or angry. What a sport!

The summer of 1947 brought new activity to tantalize a small boy's attention. Into the drought-dried pond area where the skating had taken place, a mammoth, noisy machine arrived, belching black smoke from its chimney. The machine spent a week or two pushing brush and earth around the general area where the hockey games had been played. It left a flat open area when it departed—and a sense of loss after all the captivating sights and sounds of the metal monster thrashing through the underbrush.

Then, as summer turned to fall, activity at the site resumed, and my days at the window were again filled with wonder. I watched as below me the former hockey players now returned and worked long hours with hand tools to complete the clearing of the area. They sank posts in a pattern around the edges of the open ground. Then the players nailed rough boards to the posts to form an enclosed section. Taller posts were added at intervals and floodlights mounted. Then long wires were suspended across the rink with lights hanging from them. At each of the narrower ends of the enclosed space, the men erected a wire barrier several feet above the boards. On one of the longer sides, next to a road, two access gates were installed.

By the time all of this work was completed, the first snow of the season was falling outside my window. I begged my parents to take me down to see the floodlit apparition that had grown into reality as I watched, amazed, from our apartment window.

The moment was not long in coming. For Christmas that year I received my first skates. Double runners. Bright red. As I struggled across the icy surface, my hand held by one parent or the other, and tried to find my balance, we were edging along the outer perimeter of Rye's first hockey rink. On the rink itself, skating gloriously in their new uniforms of bright red and blue, was the town's first hockey team. This was the Rye Hockey Club, later renamed the Rye Seahawks.

These men were virtual gods to boys my age. Combat veterans, supreme athletes, representing our town against other New England "town teams." This was glory almost beyond a boy's imagining.

Only by standing on mounds made of snow shoveled off the rink and thrown over the boards could I actually see what was happening in the rink itself. Even then, I could see the players only from the waist up. Later, watching games with my father, I was sometimes able to sit on his shoulders and finally get to see what went on from the waist down in games and practices. But standing on the snow pile, I was at least able to watch the flow of the game. The occasional sight of a huge player coming past me along the boards was a thrill beyond compare.

This was also about the time that I first noticed a kind of metal cage with a net behind it at each end of the rink. In front of the cage stood a player dressed in the strangest, most awkward-looking equipment. The equipment included a stick so outsized that it seemed useless for playing or passing or shooting.

My father explained that this player was the last line of defense—the man who tried to keep the other team from scoring. He was called a goalie. I thought *goalie* a very funny-sounding word. *Go-lee?*

That winter our new team played several spirited games against other area town teams, Portsmouth and Hampton among them. The Seahawks played well and usually won. One of the Rye team's strengths was that the men had played together since they were boys, including time in grade school on an informal team, the Rye Rangers. Such familiarity gave a considerable advantage in a sport as fast as hockey. I wanted very much to play on a modern edition of the Rye Rangers.

By any measure, the Seahawks' inaugural season brought success. Two dozen scrappy World War II veterans had created a hockey club, built a rink, outfitted and equipped themselves, and fought their way to a winning season, completely on their own. They even had money in the bank, thanks to a five-dollar contribution from each club member and donations from many townspeople, plus bake sales, knitting sales, and other creative fund-raising efforts by the players' wives. Hundreds of fans had cheered the team in its battles on ice. Busloads followed the team to its away games. Admittedly, the team owed some of its success to the times. The only competing entertainment was a good book or the AM radio. The nearest movie theater was a distant eight miles away, and it showed the same film for weeks at a time.

The next year brought change to the Seahawks. Through my four-year-old hockey fanatic's eyes, the change was all for the good. The two other local teams, the nearby City of Portsmouth and Town of Hampton, had excellent hockey clubs but not quite as good as the Seahawks. Over the summer of 1947, the veterans who made up the bulk of the rosters on each club talked about the future. They decided to move a handful of the better players from Hampton and Portsmouth to Rye in the interest of producing a single strong team capable of challenging the best hockey clubs around. Following this consolidation, the Portsmouth and Hampton clubs folded.

With the 1947–1948 season began the golden era of the Rye Seahawks, when they played equal to some of the great hockey teams of northern New England: Laconia, Manchester, Berlin, Amesbury, Lynnfield, Gloucester, Biddeford, Wolfeboro, Dover, Ogunquit, Westbrook, Melrose, Newburyport, Danvers, Suncook, Beverly, Weymouth. Rye's hockey team did this for well over a decade as a small, rural town on the New Hampshire seacoast, and as a team wholly self-organized and without corporate, municipal, or other institutional backing. The players did this all themselves.

Time has not erased the remarkable achievements of the Rye Seahawks through that long-ago decade. The press covered many of the exciting games, accounts that have been preserved in newspaper archives. More than a dozen of the original players, though now of considerable age, have eagerly contributed their recollections in interviews and letters. A compendium of their stories and memories will bring to the reader some sense of what amateur hockey—"town team" hockey—looked like in the mid-twentieth century, a point almost sixty years ago and about half a century after the sport first began to be widely played throughout Canada and then the United States. Further insights relating to the initial organization and development of the team are provided by personal records and memorabilia that have been preserved by players' families. These records show that those who initially brought to life the club and rink deserve great credit for the strength, vitality, and endurance of their unique endeavor.

To go out to a Seahawks game with my parents, particularly at night under the floodlights, was to hear the sharp sounds of the game—blades on ice, pucks striking sticks and boards, bodies hitting each other, a referee's whistle, the cheering townspeople. The sights were equally vivid—cars alongside the rink with headlights on, the spectacle of brightly colored uniforms, huge piles of snow outside the boards, the crowd of fans. It was overwhelming to me then and has remained vividly in memory since.

The winter of 1947–1948 was my final season as an "only child" in our family. My baby sister arrived the following spring. It was also the last winter before our family moved out of the Grey Gull to a home on nearby Grove Road (now Big Rock Road). I could think of only one thing that winter as I said my prayers before going to bed each night: "Dear Lord, when I grow up, please let me be a Rye Seahawk. *Please!*"

We are always well advised to take care in what we pray for.

2

HARD KNOCKS AND HARSH GLORY

The way out is through.
—Carl Jung

*F*ast-forward to 1958. The four-year-old we left in 1948 praying fiercely that he would one day play as a Rye Seahawk is now fourteen. He is a *Portsmouth Herald* paperboy, a Panther Patrol leader in Rye's Boy Scout Troop 181, a freshman at Portsmouth High School. He is a decent two-way hockey player in local pond scrums but an above-average goaltender in informal scrimmages organized by the town's skating elders, a few of whom play for the Seahawks.

The stage is set for wish fulfillment.

Always competitive, Rye's hockey squad has followed the arc of many other athletic teams. After reaching their apogee in the 1950–51 season, and playing for New England and New Hampshire championships in the Boston Garden that year, the core of the original team remained together through the 1952–53 season and, with that core, the winning aura and record.

But by the mid-1950s, the demands of age, family, and career began to silently steal the team's talent. One after another the players who had made special contributions to the long, successful record departed. Many of those who stayed "lost a step," in the argot of the game. Meanwhile, other New England teams competing with Rye had more rapidly attracted younger, better players. The effects were telling. By 1958, the Seahawks could not sustain a winning record against top opponents. They cast about for a solution.

Seahawk's home game, 1958–59. The author is in net.

That solution turned out to be a lifetime memory for four youngsters in their mid-teens, including me. Brought onto the team as new blood were Rye schoolboy players John Clifford at center, Jim Philbrick at wing, and Lenny Goyette on defense; I tended goal. All four of us had learned the game from Seahawks players from near infancy, and been scrimmaged and instructed by them every winter of our lives. But playing as regulars on the town team of combat veterans twice our age was another matter. We were living in a "No, ma'am" and "Yes, sir" era, and the thought of playing on a team with grown *men*—war heroes—and genuine *Seahawks*, dressed in their bold red and blue jerseys, was almost beyond belief.

Each of us four youngsters had a unique cross to bear as we made the transition from devil-may-care youth hockey player to Seahawk. My transition as a goaltender I believed to be the most difficult.

I faced a daunting challenge. The team had no other goalie. There was no one to hide behind, and no one to relieve me when I turned into a human sieve—or, perish the thought, took a puck to the face. One goaltender on a team was simply the custom at that time. As vital as goalies are to the outcome of every game, clubs at every level carried only one. Until the late 1950s, in the National Hockey League, an injury to a netminder often produced a request for a fan from the stands to put on the pads and man the vacant net for the remainder of the game.

Portsmouth's Barney Laughlin had been the Rye team's goal-tender for two years, but he was leaving for Holy Cross College. Barney gave me a few coaching sessions and then to the firing line I skated. Some may recall the movie *How Green Was My Valley*. That's what the Seahawks had—the greenest netminder (named Valley) in all of New England.

Equipment? I can only smile at what passed for goaltend-ing "equipment" in the 1940s and 1950s. A young goaltender in today's game would probably pass out cold if he was asked to enter a game dressed as we were.

First, and most critically, the head: Nothing. No helmet and no mask. No head, face, or neck protection at all. Although today this appears mindless, it was simply the custom of the time. During the 1958 NHL season, netminder Jacques Plante, playing for the New York Rangers, refused to go back in goal unless he could wear a practice face mask after a puck sliced into his face. His coach argued vehemently against such a demonstration of public cowardice but Plante stood his ground. In doing so, he overnight changed the game for all goaltenders but, regrettably, too late for my front teeth and right eyebrow. Within a year, goaltenders at every level were routinely wearing face or head protection, which, though primitive in comparison to today's fully protective helmets, reduced the number of facial and head injuries.

Second, the upper body. We typically wore a baseball catch-er's chest protector. This equipment afforded no upper-arm or shoulder protection and the body registered every shot. Many of us used a catching glove similar to a first baseman's mitt, often with a little extra padding. I fashioned my first Seahawks catching glove out of my Rye Pony League first baseman's mitt with half of my mother's dishwashing drain board folded into a roll and attached to it with rawhide to offer protection from wrist to elbow. The stick-side blocker pad and glove were also rudimentary.

Third, hockey pants. Goalies wore the same pants, athletic supporter, and protective cup as regular players wore. But I joined the Seahawks in the relatively forgiving pre–slap shot era, when a goaltender faced primarily wrist shots, snap shots, and, most menacing, the threat of obscured backhanders, where the shooter's body hid most or all cues to the direction and velocity of the coming shot. In time, every goalie learned to stitch extra foam or football pads wherever possible inside his pants to minimize bruising. Years later, goalie pants were manufactured with far better protection, including padded coverage of the spine. But not in the 1950s.

Fourth, lower-leg goalie pads. The Seahawks pads, argu- ably one reason for at least some goals scored against us, were of vintage-1930s construction. Their white canvas fabric actually wrapped around the leg and therefore did not present a large square surface target to ward off shots, as do present-day pads. However, these lightweight, comfortable pads allowed me to flop around or get up and down easily. They also provided a form of low comedy. Due to the pads' age and numerous rips and tears from sticks and skate blades, the horsehair stuffing would slowly litter the ice during a game, leaving the crease filled with a layer of fine brown fur by the final whistle.

Fifth, skates. In this one area, excellent protection had been developed early for goalies. By the 1930s, famed hockey manu- facturer Canadian Cycle & Motor (CCM) was producing a heav- ily armored boot that prevented injury and a thick, stainless-steel blade that only the rarest hard shots could bend. High prices, however, kept these skates out of reach for amateurs and blue- collar types. Goal skates cost three or four times more than a pair of standard hockey skates. Most goalies, including me, remedied the pricing problem by playing net in normal hockey skates. In pre–slap shot days, hard shots rarely bruised or injured a goalie's foot. Also, the leg pads' lower edges, which overlapped the skates almost to the ice and covered all the way to the toe, helped protect both the upper foot and its sides. Still, goalies would occasionally take a shot on the toe and have a blackened or broken toe or toes for weeks.

Sixth, the goal stick or paddle, as it is called. Goalie sticks have actually changed very little over the decades, although they are now manufactured of fiberglass or light composite materials. Players' sticks, on the other hand, evolved significantly in the modern era through exaggerated blade twist and strong light composites to produce devastatingly high puck velocity and extreme shot "heaviness," greatly increasing the workload and danger for netminders. Although both players' and goaltenders' sticks in the 1950s could have varying "lies"—that is, the stick handle's steepness or angle upward from the horizontal ice—the blades themselves were flat, as opposed to the highly curved sticks preferred by most players and goalies today.

Laughably, my first Seahawks goalie stick consisted of a standard Northland Pro skater's stick, discarded because the blade had been broken. To this I attached a homemade paddle of marine plywood scrap, with brass wood screws and several rolls of tape. My custom-made paddle made it through the first season—barely. For the second season, the team purchased two goal sticks at five dollars each, a small fortune at the time. Today, a lightweight composite goaltender's paddle can exceed two hundred dollars.

With this odd assortment of goaltending equipment, I reported to my first Seahawks practice one evening after dinner, and was told to "go get between the pipes" for the warm-up. I did as I was told, watching a line of veteran players form at the blue line, each with a puck on his stick and a gleam in his eye.

What can I say looking back on that night? Did I survive? Of course. I had to survive. The team had no other goalie. Did a lot of pucks go into the net? Yes. My teammates were veteran players in their prime, fast and shifty. Knowing. Dangerous anywhere in the offensive zone, they had head fakes, body moves, and stick dekes I had never imagined when they got close to the net. Worst of all, they had a sense of patience that I had yet to learn—of how to best use that final moment to maximum advantage before taking their shot.

Again and again, I victimized myself by committing too early, only to see a crafty smile, a quick move, and another puck deposited into the twines. I was grateful when the practice session ended and we all took laps. We then shoveled the ice (no Zambonis in those days) and flooded the chopped-up surface from a nearby fire hydrant. As one of the rookies on the team, I was to become very familiar with those two jobs. To my surprise, some of the older veterans came by to whack my pads with their sticks and to offer encouraging words.

The tears came later, as I walked home in the dark, pads and skates slung over my shoulders, equipment bag hanging from the paddle. I have learned over the ensuing decades that the harshest judgment a goaltender ever receives for his play comes from himself.

Within days of the first practice, leaving no time to do more than chew my nails and lose sleep, the first weekday-night game arrived. No more facing only my teammates' shots. Instead we would compete with veteran players of another club from another town. The enemy. And they were not coming to the Rye rink to play and lose.

❖ ❖ ❖

Game night was colder than cold, the air and stars suspended in a frozen blackness above the hanging strings of lightbulbs and corner floodlights over the rink. As I slid off the bench and onto the ice, adjusting my equipment, I noticed how many had come to watch the game. Townspeople were ringed around the boards. Beyond them were their cars, parked along the two roads that bordered the rink. It felt as if the entire town was there watching.

I manned the goal and took the warm-up. It seemed that every practice shot wound up in the net, some having passed right through me to do so. I could not stop a puck. I felt like vomiting but could not figure out where or how to do it with everyone watching. Dimly, beyond the circle of lights and people, I could see looming the great white mass of the Grey Gull Apartments, home for the first four years of my life.

I do not remember our opponent's name, only the green jerseys and stockings thick about the Rye goal for much of the evening. Miraculously, we won. Somehow, I saved most of the shots, including several I never saw. I sensed the close protection of my teammates, particularly the defensemen, who left few rebounds and effectively blocked the flying opponents from nearing the crease.

Still, I vividly recall some terrible moments. And choking fear. A player suddenly alone out in front. A pass from the corner arriving right on the tape of his stick. His eyes looking directly into mine. What was he thinking? Then that interminable fraction of a second until he took the shot, only to have it fly past my shoulder and just over the goal bar.

The first breakaway occurred in the second period. Ahead in the game but pressing, as was their tradition, the Rye five played deep in the opponent's zone. Suddenly a defenseman telegraphed his cross-ice pass, which was quickly intercepted by the opposing center, who was then off to the races.

As the center crossed our blue line, our slower-skating defense worked hard to get back. But they were only at the red line. I could expect no help. The skater cut fast straight at me, then suddenly veered toward the post at my right. I did not move. As he neared the crease, I edged slightly to his side to guard the post. He lowered his head, appearing to shoot, and then unexpectedly reached his stick across and to my left, trying to tuck the puck into the left corner of the net.

Too late I realized his ploy. Dropping to the ice, I flung my left pad out laterally in an attempt to block the puck. I felt and heard the *clink* on my skate blade as it made contact with the puck. Who had won the race? I turned and looked. The puck was in the net. If I live to be a hundred, I will still be able to relive every second of that play.

Like that first breakaway, I have crystal-clear memories of many other plays, and of entire games played under the lights on the Rye rink on nights so cold that the air was filled with the players' whitened breath. We younger players knew full well that years of harsh experiences at war had toughened our veteran players, and those on the opposing teams as well. A certain grimness shadowed many of our games, particularly those played against out-of-state teams from Maine and Massachusetts.

It was almost as if, in a sense, the war was still going on. The teams fought each other physically, giving no quarter, to gain advantage, not usually by fistfighting, though that did occur sometimes, but instead by the unrelenting fierceness of attack and the reacting toughness of defense. Nobody on the ice ever smiled, not even after scoring a goal. The team had none of the celebrations, group huddles, and fist-pumping seen today. Instead, it was like we were out there on the ice together on a deadly mission. We would relax, and perhaps smile, only after the game's final whistle had blown. Hockey was serious business in Rye, and throughout other New England post–World War II hockey towns.

My recollections of backstopping the Seahawk veterans remain vivid. Although legendary scoring greats such as Dick Wilson, John Carter, and Frankie Ciolek had by that time left the team, I can still see the quickness and cleverness of forwards like Phil Drake and Jack Hayes, and remember their great scoring hunger around the net. But as a fourteen year-old goalie, it is perhaps reasonable that I best remember the veteran defenders, my personal protectors, each of whom, many times every game, saved me from youthful impetuosity or inexperience.

Brothers Bill and Irving "Flash" Jenness ("Flash" because he was the slowest man on *any* ice rink) were the very image of solidity. Built square and thick, they were immovable in the crease, yet they moved others at will. I will always remember Bill Jenness stopping by the net the first night we faced the Berlin Maroons, a legendary team of fiery, long-haired, non-English-speaking French Canadians from the north of New Hampshire.

"Ever see a slap shot?" Bill queried, as if asking the time of day, in a quiet, fatherly voice.

"No," I answered as the practice pucks kept coming.

"Then you'd better step out and have a look," he said. I skated to the side boards.

At the other end of the rink, two or three of the Maroon forwards were striking at the puck with a high and violent, golflike swing. The shots looked like bullets, some passing right through the chicken-wire barricade behind the goal. I did not know what to say. It suddenly seemed probable that my life would end sometime that night.

Instead, although we lost 10-2, a woeful score that stood as my personal worst for forty-eight years, I never touched or was touched by a Maroons slap shot all night. A brand-new shooting concept, but not yet accurate, the pucks off the sticks of these early practitioners flew wildly in all directions. Although I prepared for death every time one of these new "slap-shooters" wound up and fired, often from near the red line, none of the shots came even close to the goal. Most flew off into the night over both net and barricade, one or two striking a parked car.

Others in the defense corps helped as well. The tall and taciturn Leighton Remick, who at age twenty had been the youngest player on the original 1946 team, quietly pointed out ways to improve my game, usually after he scored against me in a scrimmage. In my second year, after my goaltending style had lost much of its early humility, gained no little teenage arrogance, and even a touch of fury—a fury that would become my trademark through decades in net—I had developed an irritating habit of smashing my stick over the goal bar when burned by what I thought to be a soft (stoppable) goal. And in my immaturity at the time, I thought *anything* that got by me was soft. It was Leighton who gently advised me after one game that the club could not afford any more five-dollar goal sticks. If I broke another one, he said, I would be playing the rest of the season with the same type of stick used by the rest of the team. I got the point.

Have you ever entered a pasture where a large bull was grazing? Many boys growing up in Rye sought this experience as a rite of passage—to cross a pasture with a bull in it while a gang of chums watched. If you have experienced this, then you know that Rule 1 is always to keep at least one eye on the huge animal, however docile or sleepy he may appear. Rule 2 is to manage the geometry so that you always have much less distance to the nearest fence than does the bull to the seat of your pants.

Playing hockey against Rye defenseman Bob Lovett was a task equal in drama and danger to confronting a bull. A sports legend in our town, Bob had made a prep school varsity football team as its offensive center in the years after the war weighing no more than 170 pounds. But weight is not everything. At some energy level, ferocity tells. Bob, though mild in appearance off-ice, became a terror once he stepped on it. A genuine fire-breather.

With Lovett on patrol, a goalie could almost relax. Opposing players in our end were seldom looking toward the crease trying to score. Instead they were, like the boy in the field with the bull, trying to stay out of harm's way while appearing to be part of the game. Bob Lovett was that intimidating.

During one night game, a burly centerman had been roughing me up through the first two periods. Early in the third period, I stopped a shot and covered the rebound with my glove. The big center leaned in, making contact with me and poking at the puck under my glove. Referee Jack Sweetzer called for a face-off at one of the near circles.

As the players skated to their positions for the face-off, Bob quietly asked the center, "Do you know how old that goalie is?" The center grunted something back. Lovett, breathing harshly, continued. "He's fourteen. If you touch him again tonight, I will kill you." All had heard but no one spoke. Then the referee broke the shocked and frozen tableau, dropped the puck, and play continued. The opposing center did not enter our zone for the rest of the game. Sometimes, the deepest truth is clearly understood from just a few unambiguous words.

But recalling Lovett's on-ice fierceness brings to mind another, equally effective side of him. Perhaps no one in Rye's history ever gave more hours to instructing young people in sports than did Bob Lovett. This does not imply that his instruction was undemanding, in keeping with the nature of the man. What you learned at the feet of Bob Lovett—quite often literally at his feet—you retained forever.

❖ ❖ ❖

Boys growing up in Rye in the 1950s were blessed by the great quality and breadth of adult sports supervision. Seahawk center

John Clifford once observed that it was as if each boy had fifty fathers to teach him sports. His own father, Jim Clifford, was certainly one of them. Not only in hockey but also in baseball, basketball, football, and soccer, a multitude of men would teach us the rudiments of the sport or activity. They would then beat our pants off at the game just to show us what we did not know.

Rye boys had one other singular athletic outlet unavailable to those in other towns. It was Saint Francis Friary, populated by about a hundred young brothers, each of whom had apparently once been an all-state or All-American athlete in some sport, to judge by their prowess. Playing basketball and hockey against them was an exercise in futility. Facing these friars as schoolboys was as difficult, we believed, as playing against Boston's Bruins or Celtics professionals. Those dark-robed, earnest young men, so quiet, so modest, so "peace-loving," delivered absolute carnage on court and pond. There was never any "turn the other cheek" in those games. Instead they favored a strictly Old Testament–style of brutally effective play.

Still, we learned a lot playing the friars. And there was probably no better preparation on earth for becoming a Seahawk. Or an adult.

No discussion of a youthful hockey career would be complete without recounting the physical mishaps endured, particularly given the vintage equipment and lack of head and face protection. Luckily, boys of that time were formed of a material akin to case-hardened steel. In two years as a Seahawk, I never received a physical injury that kept me out of a game. Of course, I had many bumps and pulls and bruises. But those, like the constant blossoming of dark blue "goalie tattoos" on upper arms, neck, chest, and stomach, were more or less the common rewards of playing the game in that era.

I did have two significant facial injuries. Considering the hundreds of near misses while playing barefaced, I should consider myself fortunate. The worst, eating a player's unintentional stick while he was following through and up on a doorstop backhander, required eighty stitches in my lips and mouth and removed several top and bottom front teeth. The medical attention had to wait until I finished the last ten minutes of the game. I gave myself first aid by wedging bubble gum in the holes where the teeth had been.

The other facial injury occurred during a weeknight practice. Some Rye practice games could be more lively than real games. An inter-squad scrimmage was under way. My crease was seeing plenty of action. It seemed like one long, uninterrupted power play. A puck flew in from a sharp angle, which I knocked down but could not control. Immediately, Seahawks from both scrimmage teams were fighting for the rebound in the crease. Several fell on top of me in the struggle, pinning both my hands and arms. Still looking for the puck, I saw that it had been pushed out to the opposing left defenseman, Rick Oeser. He quickly fired a hard wrist shot at the mostly open net above the struggling men. Instead, the puck came directly at my head. I saw it coming at my lower face but was held fast by the pileup. At the last moment, I lowered my head as much as I could. The puck struck hard above the right eyebrow. A momentary lights-out feeling, then a rush of pain. Blood in the crease. Plenty of it. A towel to cover my face, and hands helping me off the ice.

John Clifford's father, a spectator that night, drove me to Portsmouth Hospital to receive my hockey badge of honor—eighteen stitches. Though not incurred in a game, this injury caused one of only three incidences in a playing career spanning fifty-six years that I did not finish a session in goal.

In the autumn of 2007, I had finished interviewing all former Seahawks players still living on the New Hampshire seacoast. I then began conducting telephone interviews with all former Seahawks living elsewhere for whom contact information was available. I came to the name Rick Oeser of Spokane, Washington, and paused.

Would he recall that cold night and the bloody injury after fifty years? After all, he had not been on the receiving end. I looked again at Rick's name on my roster. Finally I dialed the number.

"Hello?" I heard.

"Rick Oeser—formerly of Rye, New Hampshire?" I asked.

"Yes, that's me."

"This is Bruce Valley. We played some hockey together on the Rye town team back in the fifties. I'd like to interview you and get some of your memories and recollections for a book I'm writing about the Seahawks."

Silence.

"Rick?"

Longer silence.

"Rick? . . ."

Finally, "You know, I must have waited twenty-five or thirty years after that night for your parents to sue me."

Had I heard him correctly? "What?" I asked again.

"Yup, after I caught you over the eye and opened you up in that practice game, I just knew they were going to sue."

Stunned, I considered for a moment, then said: "Rick, that would never have happened. My parents never sued anyone in their lives. The cut was an *accident*. You shot for the open goal. I was pinned down and couldn't move, and so caught the puck. End of story."

"You mean you're not angry about it?"

"Nope. Never have been."

I told Rick that during my time in the Navy, the medical people had wanted to operate because the eyelid hangs a bit from scar tissue. I turned down the operation. I've grown to like that eyebrow. It makes a statement. Someone might think I'm a former boxer and leave me alone.

"Well, okay then. I guess I can let it go as well."

And he did, and we had an excellent interview.

The magic of hockey—and common memory—across time and space.

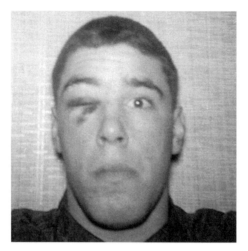

Author at fourteen with stitched right eyebrow.

3

SUMMER HOCKEY

People are inexterminable.

—Robert Frost

*P*hil Drake used to hold a luncheon at the Rye Beach Club for former Seahawks team members in mid-summer every other year. The last was in July 2006. There will be no more. Phil died in the fall of 2007.

Only a handful of the players could make the event in 2006, though perhaps a dozen still lived in the area. Phil hosted Frankie Ciolek, John "Peanut" Culliton, and Jack Hayes from the original 1940s team. John Clifford, Gordie Gaskell, and I represented the younger generation of schoolboy players who had joined the team in the late 1950s.

The fare was simple—hot dogs, potato chips, and Coke—for the event would be about friendship and reminiscences, not food. Aware that I had recently begun research and was conducting interviews for a book about their team, the former players were more animated than usual. The air was thick with anecdotes and recollections of games played more than half a century ago. A portable tape recorder captured the tales.

As the players gruffly enjoyed the welcoming jokes and jibes, I noticed something about the men. Although the original Seahawks were all well into their eighties (player-coach Dave Boise was a remarkable ninety-five but ailing that day and could not attend; nor could Leighton Remick for similar reasons); they were not, in

Dave Boise, Seahawks' player-coach, at age ninety-five.

the flesh, old men as that term is normally understood. Their eyes were alive with energy. Their recollections were almost unnervingly sharp. Energized by active memories, they looked ready to put on skates and play the game.

We spent an hour eating lunch, exchanging pleasantries, and reliving a number of Seahawks games against tough 1950s hockey clubs. Finally, it felt right to introduce something I had discovered in my research. I pulled out a newspaper clipping of an exciting game the Seahawks had *not* won on January 17, 1951. Although the Rye team had staged a furious four-goal comeback against a very competitive club from Gloucester, Massachusetts, and finally tied, we ultimately lost.

The play-by-play write-up in the following day's *Portsmouth Herald* described the Seahawks falling behind by three goals in

Leighton Remick, the youngest original Seahawk, in his eighties.

the early going, then rallying late in the third period to tie the game with Frankie Ciolek and Peanut Culliton scoring on brilliant individual efforts. Then Phil Drake took a desperate penalty bringing down Gloucester's best forward on a breakaway. In the game's closing seconds, Gloucester scored the winning goal with Rye still a man short.

As I finished reading the game summary, there was a brief silence, then an argument broke out among the three old players—Phil Drake, Frankie Ciolek, and Peanut Culliton. The penalty was necessary! No, it wasn't! The earlier individual goals had broken Gloucester's spirit and they were finished! No, they weren't! On and on it went, men no longer old, each recalling the details of that long-ago game.

I interrupted. "Notice something?" I asked. The arguing stopped. Heads turned, eyes questioning. "In this game, played fifty-five years and six months ago, everyone mentioned in the article is here today sitting at this table. Just what are the chances?"

The point took hold. They stared at each other, then off into the distance, savoring the irony and the blessing inherent in that statement. There we sat, we lovers of hockey, debating the game's

The Rye Beach Club Seahawks' luncheon, July 2006. Four original players—
Frankie Ciolek, Jack Hayes, Phil Drake, and John "Peanut" Culliton—at center;
second-generation players, John Clifford, left, and Gordie Gaskell, right.

details with those who had actually been there and distinguished themselves in that event played so long ago. An amazing moment for us all.

Then as I looked across the table at the four men who had renewed the animated discussion of their roles in that ageless hockey game, something strange happened, perhaps a warping of the space-time continuum. Suddenly the years stripped away from the old-timers. Their hair thickened and darkened. Facial creases smoothed. I blinked, swallowed hard, and looked past my old friends to the white sands of Rye Beach, the blue Atlantic, the Isles of Shoals outlined on the far offshore horizon. What was happening? I was drinking Coca-Cola—straight!

❖ ❖ ❖

Had I closed my eyes? Suddenly it was not balmy but very cold. My shorts and polo shirt had been replaced by a heavy coat, scarf, cap, and gloves. I was standing on a snow bank. *CRACK!* Looking across the rink boards, I watched as smooth-skating Rye Seahawks defenseman Harlan Carter—a powerful young man with wavy blond hair—collided with a Gloucester player, delivering an expert hip check, driving him into the boards and to the ice.

Rangy defenseman Leighton Remick swooped in swiftly, deftly picking the puck from between the two downed players and snapping a perfect up-rink pass to a sprinting Phil Drake, blond head bent low, skates flashing side to side as he accelerated. A quick headman pass to Jack Hayes, another speedster, found the puck at center ice. Entering the offensive zone with speed, Hayes dropped the puck for Drake, who, moving laterally, drew both defensemen to him.

A quick backhand saucer pass directly to the tape on winger Frankie Ciolek's stick sent him in alone, straight up the middle. The Gloucester goalie had just seconds to make his move. As Ciolek neared, the defender quickly dove to the ice, stretching out his pads, waving his catching glove as a distraction. Ciolek deked left and spun smoothly to his right. Then all in one motion, he lifted the puck high into the net. *Score!*

The Rye players turned and skated back to center ice. There was no celebration. The team was still two goals behind and it was well into the third period. There was work to be done on this frigid January evening in 1951.

❖ ❖ ❖

The dream state passed. The images slowly faded and with them the intense cold. The summer's warmth returned. The men sitting across from me were once again in their late eighties. Their eyes, however, shone with that same excitement and great love for hockey I had seen in my reverie, suggesting there may be in man essential elements that never grow old. Had I been dreaming? Or had I seen something real? I looked down at my arms. Despite the heat and humidity, the telltale rash of goose bumps answered my question.

Team photo taken in 1948. Courtesy of the Portsmouth Herald *and Mrs. Priscilla Jenness. Back row, left to right: Stuart Wright, Frank Ciolek, Irving "Flash" Jenness, Guy Kelsey, John Carter, Leighton Remick, William "Bill" Jenness, Phil Goss, and John Carberry. Front row, left to right: John "Jack" Hayes Jr., Harlan Carter, Dick Peyser, John "Peanut" Culliton, player-coach Dave Boise, and Dick Wilson. Note the snow piles behind the players and sideboards from shoveling the rink clear of snow.*

4

NEW ENGLAND TOWN HOCKEY TEAM

Autumn, yes, winter was in the wind.
—Robert Frost

*T*he tales and legends of Rye's post–World War II hockey team that come down to us over generations of telling and retelling, mostly untrue, are exceeded only by the team's actual achievements.

The Seahawks did not win the New England or New Hampshire amateur championships in the early 1950s, as has been rumored. But they did twice play in those championships at the Boston Garden. They did not play against semipro teams. But they did on occasion play against college teams. Several of the many town clubs they played, particularly in Massachusetts, were composed largely of ex-college all-stars and former Olympians.

The Seahawks' greatest achievement, however, is that they built something solid and memorable from scratch with their own hands and with negligible external support, fostered its growth for almost fifteen years, and did all this at a competitive playing level that has kept them in the active memory of both the town and the New Hampshire seacoast region for half a century.

These men came from a small town perched on the Atlantic seacoast. They grew up during the Great Depression, when hardship was common and hope was rare. They had seen neighbors and families lose jobs and homes. They learned to expect little from life, and to deal with the future one day at a time.

Original Rye Seahawks wool hockey sweater (courtesy of Dick Lilly).

Then, just as the world seemed to return to normal, with the weight of the Depression lessening, the Japanese attack on Pearl Harbor, on December 7, 1941, shattered the image of America as a bastion of safety. Millions of men set aside their normal lives and put on uniforms to defend their country.

At a time when they would normally have had their lives filled with the frivolous, with young love and school and first jobs, American men were instead fighting across Europe and Asia, in the Atlantic and the Pacific, against two of the most ruthless military powers the world had ever known. Many were gone for four years. Some for five. Some forever.

Then the fighting ended. Men came home to resurrect their former lives. Given what they had seen, done, and survived, their time for frivolity had long passed. Mature beyond their years and tempered by combat, the men used the discipline they had learned in the ranks to begin rebuilding their lives.

But this generation that gave so much found America unprepared for their return, unready to help them move forward. Jobs, money, automobiles—all were scarce. The hundred or so combat veterans returning to their families in Rye were put into what was euphemistically called the 52-20 Club, a federal program that provided twenty dollars each week for fifty-two weeks, or until the veteran found a job.

What to do with the time on their hands, and the need to share the experiences and complex feelings each man had about the war, something impossible to do with those who had not fought? The answer in Rye turned out to be pond hockey, informal play without goals or side boards, as the veterans gathered in the winter of 1946–1947 on a pond at the corner of Myrica Avenue and Ocean Boulevard.

For many who played daily on the pond, finding solace in the activity and in the company of fellow combat veterans, this was not their introduction to the game. Just before the war had begun, in 1940–1941, the Rye Hockey Club, a volunteer organization, was formed to provide a town rink for community skating and hockey instruction. Locals Ed Herlihy and Dick Locke taught Rye's junior high youngsters how to play hockey, passing along the rudimentary skills of the game and introducing the boys to team play. Eventually, an informal youth team was formed with these seventh- and eighth-grade students. The team was called the Rye Rangers.

The Rangers occasionally played supervised games against a Portsmouth youth team on the South Playground pond, and also against a team from east Rye. Though the rink and team were both set aside after the attack on Pearl Harbor, the core of the Rye Rangers and their individual and team skills later laid the foundation for the Seahawks. These former Rye Rangers, now combat veterans, became the stalwarts who created the Rye team, then carried it for fifteen years, from its first game in 1946 until its last in 1960.

One expects to find in military-trained men qualities of organization, drive, and discipline. Rye's veterans certainly had those attributes. In 1946, the pond hockey players started to talk of getting organized and challenging other local teams—particularly that of the nearby city of Portsmouth, which already had a team of veterans sponsored by its VFW chapter, and that of Hampton to the south.

One weekend evening four Rye veteran players met in the Normandy Bar, a favorite vets hangout in nearby Salisbury Beach, a Massachusetts seaside town famous as a century-old carnival, honky-tonk, and amusement center. That meeting yielded a plan to organize a town team and eventually construct an open-air ice rink. Phil Drake was the natural leader, spark plug, and driving force. Bill Jenness served as the administrator. Leighton Remick and Jack Hayes rounded out the key organizers.

Though most official and unofficial records of the Seahawks were lost decades ago to fire, we fortunately have the original, handwritten organizing records of the team kept by Bill Jenness. From these it is possible to review the initial outfitting of the team and follow their plan to construct a rink.

Bill Jenness's records begin:

Rye Hockey Association
Membership Fee: $5.00

Which entitles you to play on the team and use the rink for scrimmages and skating privileges.

Also each member will be called upon to do his share in keeping the rink in condition.

Uniforms:
The club will have 12 complete uniforms.

Anyone having one is to be responsible for it, and no one can keep it if he is not playing in the scheduled games. Unless you wish to buy your own. Furnish your own shin pads and gloves.

Injuries:
The club will not be responsible for any player who becomes injured while playing for the club.

Club Directors:
Harlan Carter
Leighton Remick
Bill Jenness
Phil Goss
Phil Drake

Jenness's record goes on to report progress in the late 1947 time frame:

Progress of the Club to date

We have the pond with permission of the owner to do as we wish. The pond is in front of the Grey Gull Apartments, which is handy to both light and water.

Boards we have had given to us by Alex Brown. They were originally the floors of the National Guard Camp at Rands Field. They aren't new but will do until we have funds to purchase something better. The rink will be 160 by 65, which is a legal rink size. The boards will be four feet high in sections of nine and sixteen feet.

The support posts are already in place and we are now waiting for the final freeze to start with the boards. We have support posts every nine feet on the ends and every fifteen feet on the sides.

Lights:

We have the lights and some wire which was purchased last winter when trying to flood the tennis courts at Abenaqui Golf Club. The only thing we need is more wire, which can support the lights over the rink. We have fifteen 150 watt flood bulbs, which equals 2250 watts for an area of 10,400 sq. ft. We have four light poles and need four more. Ea. 22 ft.

Snow Scrapers:

We have five snow scrapers.

The report concludes with a summary of the club's financial status and expenditures. All players had indeed contributed their five dollars, with Bill Moulton adding an extra five. In addition, several members of the Rye community contributed to the team. Among them were Everett Bixby, Sam Allen, Harold Hixon, Norman Jenness, Fred Dodge, Abbott Drake, Frank Wilson Sr., Norman Rand, Neal Philbrick, Clint Gaskell, and Betty Smith, along with newspaper publisher J. D. Hartford, who later supplied the team with leather head protectors.

A list of all players who competed for the Rye Seahawks may be found in appendix A. Input for these names comes from Bill Jenness's records and his original spiral notebook assigning jersey numbers to members of the founding team in 1946–1947. Also useful were news clippings, interviews, and other reliable sources. Some of those on the early lists of players may never have actually suited up to play for the team in games, though they appear in team pictures and likely practiced with the squad.

. Bill Jenness's historical documents are helpful for another, more vital purpose. Given the loss of the team's official records, Bill's papers provide the only written data regarding the team in the two years (1946–1948) before local newspapers began to report on the Seahawks, in the 1948–1949 season.

The records indicate that, entering the 1947–1948 playing season, as of November 20, 1947, the Seahawks had a thirty-dollar balance in the bank from the preceding year. Expenditures were primarily for rink equipment such as light sockets, floodlights, wire, and electricity (lights). The record also uncovers an interesting early business custom of the town hockey teams. Cash guarantees, usually ten dollars, were put up to ensure that the visiting team would show up to play. Then, according to records, a hat would be passed at the game. The proceeds were split between the teams and the guarantee money returned. Typical proceeds given to the Seahawks for their games ranged from nine to twenty-five dollars.

The records regarding guarantees and game proceeds also provide the sole information available on which teams played the Seahawks in its first two seasons. Portsmouth, Dover, Biddeford, Westbrook, Newburyport, Melrose, and Wolfeboro were the opponents.

One of the largest expenditures in the first year was for uniforms and equipment. R. D. McDonough Sporting Goods, of Portsmouth, received the bulk of these orders, totaling about $250 for the first two years. An undated invoice from John B. Varick Company is included in the records and is presumably from the same era. It is shown below so that those who purchase hockey equipment in the modern era can see what hockey equipment, and particularly goalkeeper's equipment, was selling for in 1946–1947.

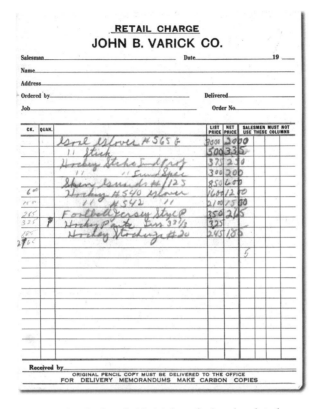

John B. Varick invoice for Seahawks' initial outfitting (undated, presumably early 1947).

❖ ❖ ❖

The Seahawks' first official game against a visiting team is reported to have taken place in early January 1947. The opponent was the Portsmouth VFW team. The teams played on Myrica Pond, with makeshift goals and no side or end boards. Rye's new town hockey team won its first game, and most of the remaining games of early 1947, before an early thaw ended the season.

From the first official game comes a story that is at once the most comical and the most embarrassing in Seahawks lore. The club had worked overtime to ensure that it had proper uniforms and equipment to face a Portsmouth VFW team expensively decked out in new uniforms from their sponsor. But as game

*Rare photos of the Rye Hockey Club's first official game in early
January 1947 against the Portsmouth VFW team. Note the vintage
player equipment, homemade goals and rough lumber sideboards.
Photo:* Portsmouth Herald

day neared, the Seahawks lacked one vital item to complete the
uniform—garter belts to hold up the long stockings. No sport shop
had any in stock. The team convened an emergency meeting to
discuss the crisis. Panicky phone calls produced no leads. It was
an impossible situation. Shin pads required stockings to be prop-
erly placed for protection. The stockings would not stay up by
themselves. Finally, a never-to-be-named Seahawk was directed
to go to the women's lingerie department at a local store and do
the best he could.

*Prime organizer, Phil Drake on the Seahawks' rink,
the Grey Gull Apartments in background. Inscription
reads, "In my glory, Phil January 8, 1948."*

The result? In the Rye Seahawks' ceremonial first official
game, against the Portsmouth Vets, each player was wearing an
extra-large, bright pink ladies garter belt under his hockey pants
to hold up his stockings.

If only their opponents had known . . .

The pink garter story offers an opportunity to highlight the
significant contributions that players' wives made developing Rye's
hockey club. Although money was limited, funds were needed to
equip the team and build the rink. The players' wives addressed
that need with bake sales, quilt sales, social events, and parties for

1948 Seahawks on home ice: Bill Jenness (12), Bill Moulton (10), and
Frank Drake (3).

which tickets were sold. They were as essential as the players to
the team's success.

There was very much a sense among those involved that the
creation of the team and its rink was a cooperative effort of men
and women—that everyone was taking on the project. This may
well speak to how the Seahawks endured as a self-help enterprise
under difficult conditions for fifteen years.

The wives also shared custody of one of the team's most
important talismans: a large liquid container that the team called
"the Old Urn." Long lost to history, it was for years the means of
providing refreshment—coffee, hot chocolate, and possibly other
liquids on occasion—between the periods. Shocking.

From the end of the Seahawks' shortened 1946–47 season
to the beginning of the first full season in 1947–1948, the team
accomplished much. Notably, a full-scale regulation hockey rink
was constructed on the Myrica Pond site. In the conveniently
parched summer of 1947, which virtually dried up the pond, a
large bulldozer, reportedly provided gratis by local manufacturer
Iafolla Industries, leveled the rink area and made it much easier

for players and volunteers to burn brush, get support posts and light poles installed, and generally ready the rink area for boards as soon as ice formed in the fall. I witnessed all of this activity from an upper-floor Grey Gull Apartment window as a fascinated three-year-old.

Important personnel changes also occurred over the summer, wielding a far-reaching impact on the growth, development, and success of the Seahawks. Captain of his Yale University hockey team in the late 1930s, and with international amateur playing experience in Europe, skilled defenseman Dave Boise, of nearby North Hampton, joined the team as player-coach. He brought a much needed instructional stability to the Seahawks. Though several years older than other team members, his skills as a stolid backliner contributed to the team's on-ice success.

Also from North Hampton, young banker John Carter, a former student at Brown University (and no relation to Harlan Carter, already playing defense on the team), brought great energy and intellect, an almost reckless skating style, and a dead-eye shot to the first-line center's slot. Carter soon took over administrative management of the Seahawks, arranging games and handling press relations. He had a dental plate to replace several missing front teeth. Carter shocked fans by nonchalantly removing it and tucking it into his wife Nancy's jacket pocket just before games.

Meanwhile, the Portsmouth VFW team had unexpectedly folded. Its star winger, Dick Wilson, an almost-professional-caliber hockey player and a lethal scorer, and small-bodied but extremely capable defenseman John "Peanut" Culliton soon joined the Rye team. Gifted multisport athlete Frankie Ciolek also signed on. Ciolek, who had recently moved into town from Ipswich, in the Bay State, added another offensive dynamo to the roster.

In their first season, Rye's Seahawks had formed a solid team, capable of winning any game. Now they had the potential for greatness, and John Carter began to exploit that potential as he sought to add the most powerful northern New England hockey clubs to the Seahawks' schedule.

Somewhere in these early years, Carter's contacts to feed the press information on upcoming games led him to seek a more

specific identity for a team heretofore known only as the Rye Hockey
Club. He chose the seahawk, a fierce maritime bird of prey, as a
fitting representative for a team living and playing on the rugged
Atlantic coastline. The Rye Seahawks it was from that moment.

❖ ❖ ❖

What followed was the golden era of the Rye Seahawks hockey
club. Playing throughout New Hampshire, Massachusetts, and
Maine against the most competitive squads available—teams also
composed mainly of combat veterans of World War II and later
the Korean conflict—the Seahawks built a winning record and a
reputation for tough, fast hockey. As the seahawk is an aggressive
predator, so were the Seahawks an aggressive, predatory hockey
squad. (Appendix B lists the New England teams the Seahawks
played in those competitive years, from 1948 to 1954. Appendix C
contains a wealth of *Portsmouth Herald* news stories of memorable
games from that era. It appears that no newspaper reports were
written about the Seahawks before 1948 or after 1955.)

The rewards for aggressive team development and a consistently high level of play throughout the schedule were clearly mani-
fest in those years. By now the Seahawks had joined the Harvest
Hockey League, which played on the novel indoor artificial ice of
Lynn Arena, in Massachusetts. Playing indoors, the league could
schedule games many weeks before outdoor natural ice formed.
Players' conditioning improved. The Seahawks seasoned their
roster early by playing competitively in the Harvest League and
were in mid-season form when outdoor play began.

In 1950 the Seahawks' record brought them an invitation to
the New England Class B championships, to be played in Boston
Garden. Although the team lost in the semifinals, on April 6, 1950,
to the powerful Lynnfield Knights, it took Lynnfield the full regulation game plus *six* overtime periods to put them away. The final
score was 2-1.

The next year, 1951, was perhaps the best the Seahawks ever
played. The team produced a 4-4 record indoors and a 13-6 record
outdoors, for an overall winning record of 17-10. Over the season
the Rye team scored 142 goals and allowed just 100. They made

Seahawks' first line, 1950–51. Dick Wilson, right wing (left), John Carter (center), Frankie Ciolek, left wing (right).

it back to the Boston Garden for their final appearance there in the New Hampshire Class B championships. The Seahawks went all the way to the championship game, but lost to perennial New Hampshire powerhouse Laconia by a score of 9-4.

During the 1950–1952 seasons, the team moved its rink from the Myrica Avenue site near the beach to a field near player-coach Dave Boise's farm, at the corner of Atlantic Avenue and Woodland Road in North Hampton. Although this location had some advantages, poor drainage proved a problem and the ice could not be consistently maintained. For the 1953 season, the Seahawks returned the rink to the Myrica Avenue site, where it and the team remained for the duration.

A few more skilled players joined the Seahawks roster during the pinnacle years of 1948–1952. Local legend Bob Lovett, an offensive center in football in the late 1940s and later the primary sports instructor for a generation of Rye teenagers, in 1949 brought an almost terrifying toughness to the team's defense. But by 1955, most of the talented original core were gone. Wilson left to fly for the Air Force. Ciolek, Culliton, Peyser, John and Harlan Carter, and player-coach Dave Boise left for reasons of career and family, and probably to the growing exigencies of age.

The results were predictable. The Seahawks still competed capably against some teams but, lacking the talented players who had moved on, they had become again a good team instead of a great one. They gradually dropped out of the top tier of competitive clubs. Still, the seasons of 1955–1957 ended with favorable win-loss records. After John Carter departed, no one made the effort to schedule games against the most competitive teams. The schedule was whittled in half, to less than a dozen games, all outdoors. It helped that more local talent had made the grade to play for Rye, including several veterans of the recently ended Korean conflict. The Oeser brothers, Rick, Jim, and Bobby, added offensive punch. Gordie Gaskell brought his great height to the back line. And Portsmouth's capable Barney Laughlin took over in net.

By 1958, the team's new arrivals, together with a small band of the original 1946 team, now in their early to mid-thirties—Phil Drake, Leighton Remick, Jack Hayes, and brothers Bill and Flash Jenness—were just holding on. The wheels slowed further and the competition got younger and better. Taking note of that latter trend, the team brought local fourteen- to sixteen-year-olds up to the Seahawks: center John Clifford, winger Jim Philbrick, defenseman Lenny Goyette, and me. I replaced Barney Laughlin in net when he left for college.

The Seahawks played only a few games in the final two years of 1958 and 1959, with mixed results. Against equally talented town teams, the Seahawks' grit and experience paid off, and they usually won. The veteran players and younger but faster schoolboys proved a winning combination. But against a more talented club—two games against the legendary Berlin Maroons come immediately to mind—the Rye team was obviously outclassed and the Seahawks spent some long nights on the ice.

There were other changes by the late 1950s. Television had been transformed from novelty to commodity. Suddenly every home had one. Most of the hundreds of fans who for years had turned out to support the Seahawks found Jack Benny, Ozzie and Harriet, Milton Berle, Jackie Gleason, and Art Linkletter to be better fare. With the temperature of a comfy den in the sixties and outside in the single digits (plus or minus), it was an understandable choice.

❖ ❖ ❖

The reference to the frigid winter temperatures in the Granite State during that period remind me of one of the most challenging aspects of the Seahawks playing outdoors on natural ice. Weather always brought difficulties in ice management, and the related challenge of scheduling games around temperature, weather, and the players' obligations to work and family. The late 1940s and early 1950s were characterized by higher-than-normal snowfall and below-average temperatures. Yet even the coldest winter had brief warming periods, sometimes with rain.

The Seahawks could easily predict the general pattern of the winter season. Around Thanksgiving the ponds would form ice thick and hard enough for hockey. The players would get the rink into shape and flood the surface to smooth it. Then practices began. Sometime in late March or early April, the ice rotted and hockey ended. The four months between Thanksgiving and spring thaw brought cold but unpredictable weather, during which teams crammed into the schedule as many home and away games as possible—without e-mail, cell phones, or faxes! Sudden temperature variances and the arrival of snow or sleet necessitated flexible schedules. The need often arose to play a game each day for several days of good ice to make up for weather-canceled events.

Even when temperature and weather cooperated, preparing the ice for games took many hours of labor. Teams played most games at night and on weekends, as all of the men held day jobs, many at the Portsmouth Navy Yard in Kittery, Maine. The night before or the morning of a game, the ice had to be scraped clean, then flooded using a fire hose from a nearby hydrant. If another game was to be played the following day, the ice was scraped and flooded again immediately after the concluded game.

The Seahawks did all of this work themselves. They often practiced at dawn, went to work for the day, rushed home to eat and then to the rink to play the game, then scraped and flooded yet again, went home to bed, and got up at dawn for work—an exhausting cycle! Rink preparation was an unforgiving task in cold weather, made much worse by wind. The original Seahawks shouldered this responsibility without complaint year after year. Many kept at it for fifteen years, such was their love for the game and for the team.

Snow made things even more difficult. When it snowed, the rink had to be shoveled clean by hand—an enormous undertaking if a foot or more of snow had fallen—then scraped and flooded. The only alternative was to cancel a game.

A *Portsmouth Herald* news article of late winter 1951 illustrates the difficulties:

> After getting away to a very slow start because of the mild and uncertain weather in December and January, by January 22 Rye had played eight games, five of those being played in six days. The difficulties that confront a team relying on outdoor uncovered ice are in evidence in this early uncertain time of the season. A quick cold snap must be utilized in order to build or improve the ice surface, and yet it is often followed by several thawing days, which usually undo any work already done. This means that a team has to keep working on the rink whenever there is a cold night or day and hope that some games can be played before bad weather again appears.

The reporter continued:

> Rye encountered its best ice at Wolfeboro on two occasions, winning one and losing the other, each by the same score, 8-7. Rye's best home ice was used but not seen when they played Dover legion in a hard snowstorm. The last game against Suncook at Rye also had good ice.

With this complicated and demanding process in mind, consider that in one winter stretch of 1951 the Seahawks played twenty-one games, home and away, all outdoors, in nineteen days. And went to work on weekdays. This story would cause today's coddled hockey-playing youngsters, delivered in a warm minivan to a heated dressing room, then brought into a pristine, constant-temperature enclosed rink surface with clean sparkling ice, to ask from which planet the Seahawk aliens had come.

Enormous credit must be given to this group of men who, loving a sport uncommonly, endured for many years the sacrifices and burdens to keep it going. It would seem that these graduates of years of World War II combat and the decade of the Great Depression before it were simply a different breed of man—stronger, better, more energized and disciplined than those of us who came later. There was just no quit in them. None at all. Those of us privileged to play hockey with these men near the end of the Seahawks era have carried the standard they set for us throughout our lives. We pay tribute to them every day when we show but a fraction of their strength in the living of our lives.

❖ ❖ ❖

Everything mortal has its season.

By 1960 the Seahawks no longer existed. The original players who lasted that long probably felt relief, having reached ages when being repeatedly hit by fast-moving men and objects left a soreness that took days to go away. Some young players, like me, went off to school. Others, free of the team's demands, tried out new directions in their career. A few Seahawks found other venues to continue playing hockey.

For the next few winters, a group of former Seahawks rented the outdoor artificial rink at Phillips Exeter Academy, by then my home ice. They would gather for a friendly game or two each winter to rekindle friendships, relive the memories, and play hockey again with and against their old teammates. I scored the only highlight goal of my life during one of those games.

Playing left wing, I captured a saucer pass from the center, my childhood friend Roger Nold entering the offensive zone. I took a few quick strides and let go a no-look wrist shot that just caught the far top corner of the net. The shot beat my former netminding instructor Barney Laughlin. Fluke that it was for a goaltender to score in *any* scenario, I cherish that score to this day.

Author in net, Naval Academy Alumni game, 2006.

5

NAVY HOCKEY

I have not yet begun to fight!
—John Paul Jones

I rose from the dais to speak as president of the Friends of Navy Hockey, the U.S. Naval Academy men's hockey support and booster organization, at its annual postseason banquet one spring evening in the late 1990s. Unexpectedly, I found myself setting aside the topic I had been asked to discuss—the "old-time hockey" of my youth—and addressing instead my personal debt to the Navy team.

About a year earlier, I had incurred an apparently career-ending sports injury—not, I hasten to add, while playing hockey. In a friendly neighborhood softball game, my right knee was badly hurt in a base-running incident. The base runner slid into second with one leg raised, driving my planted right leg sideways and tearing out tendon and cartilage on both sides of the knee. Doctors recommended a complete rebuild. Wary about knee surgery success rates, I chose instead to wear a full-leg cast for months, followed by rehabilitation, in the hope of regaining enough strength and function to return to sports.

The outcome was still unknown when my wife and I accepted an invitation in late winter to visit the academy in Annapolis and watch the annual competition among the drum-and-bugle corps of all of the service academies. The civilian director of the Naval Academy corps, the "D&B," had particularly wanted my attendance because, for the competition, he had rearranged a song I had written and arranged while a midshipman at the academy. I had learned what I knew of musical writing and arranging as a member of New Hampshire's first drum-and-bugle corps, the Golden Eagles of Portsmouth, which competed throughout northern New England from 1957 to 1959.

We watched the competition from the bleachers, being careful with the cast and crutches. Each corps performed to a very high standard. But it was obvious that the Naval Academy's music and marching formations exceeded those of the competitors. Navy's corps, in fact, eventually won the trophy. The experience was emotional for me. I had no idea that my old songs had somehow remained in the unit's repertoire. Hearing them again was a powerful moment. I wiped away tears as my old unit marched from the field.

After thanking the director for including us in the event, we made our way slowly across the academy's yard toward our car. We passed venerable Dahlgren Hall, built in 1898 as a cannon training facility and used in my time for rainy-day indoor formations, pickup basketball, and the academy's legendary tea dances. There I stopped in shock.

Outside the seaward end of Dahlgren Hall hung a sign that, as I told the players, parents, coaches, and fans that night at the banquet, changed my life—or at least my athletic life.

It read:

Alumni Hockey Game—1400 [2 PM].

I looked at the sign and then at my wife. The announcement told me several things. If the academy was sponsoring an alumni hockey game, then it must have a hockey team, and, of course, a rink. All of this was new to me! Though it was past three o'clock, we hustled inside. There, where Dahlgren's dozen basketball courts used to be, gleamed a full-blown hockey rink—boards, glass, penalty boxes, lights, scoreboard—and on the ice two teams in varying colors of blue and gold were engaged in a lively game.

We watched briefly from afar. Then I hobbled to the end where a young alumni netminder was trying bravely but unsuccessfully

Author in net, Naval Academy alumni game, 2006.

to stave off a splendidly conditioned, well-coached Navy squad. It was late in the third period and play soon ended. The two teams lined up for the traditional center-ice handshake and the playing of the academy's "Navy Blue and Gold" anthem. Looking up, I saw the score, 16-3 in favor of the Navy hockey team.

Tears were again on my face but for a different reason. I had an epiphany. Watching the alumni goalie gave me an idea. While I had all but conceded that my knee injury would end my participation in many sports—tennis, touch football, and soccer—it appeared that the hockey goalie's equipment, and particularly the large leg pads, which encapsulate the leg firmly from above the knee to both heel and toe, might offer sufficient protection and stability for me eventually to return to my favorite sport.

I had not played hockey for many months. Still, on the spot I proposed my plan to my disconcerted and doubtful wife, Nancy. The cast would be removed in another six weeks. Three months of rehabilitation should restore strength and function. In the fall, I would begin skating again, then play at least weekly in pickup

Naval Academy alumni team photo. Author front row, right.

games. Before year's end I would play more frequently and competitively in local A and B league games. And the following February, one year from that day, I would play in the academy's alumni hockey game—and allow fewer goals than had been scored that day.

Astonishingly, the plan worked as advertised. I did play the following year, and every year since. I allowed three goals in the half of that first alumni game when I was back in net. The knee? It held up just fine.

As I spoke to those at the banquet, ten years after my return to hockey from the injury, I wanted them to know how important that discovery was—how satisfying the physical comeback—how grateful I felt to resume playing *our* game at an age when almost all of my contemporaries had crossed over to the other side of the glass. Had I not chanced to see that alumni sign, none of this would have happened.

❖ ❖ ❖

Like me, Navy hockey had certainly come a long way. When I first arrived, in 1962, the academy had no rink and no team. Usually, in December through February, a cold spell would freeze the reflection pool behind the library. A pickup game erupted on this makeshift rink every afternoon. We hockey stalwarts from New England among the midshipmen tried to demonstrate superior prowess on our blades to those from New York, New Jersey, Pennsylvania, Michigan, and Minnesota.

There was one obstacle, and a few of us paid dearly for it. At "center ice" an iron fountain sculpture stood about twelve inches above the surface of the ice. Early in the game, everyone remained aware of the sculpture and skated clear, much as we had done in avoiding obstacles frozen on ponds when growing up. But late in the game, with egos and passions flaring, the sculpture would be forgotten until someone struck it unawares. Several broken ankles resulted.

Later, in the early 1970s, when the sculpture-dodging midshipmen of my era were for the most part serving overseas in the heat and humidity of Vietnam and the South China Sea, a group of midshipmen, led by Mel DeMars, received permission to organize officially and begin playing in an amateur league in nearby Baltimore. The Naval Academy superintendent's wife was an avid hockey fan, so the rest of the story is history. Within a year, a rink had been purchased and installed in Dahlgren Hall, which just happened to be located directly across from the superintendent's quarters. Navy hockey had a home.

Navy Hockey is now officially thirty-eight years old. The team remains a club organization, currently playing in the Eastern States Collegiate Hockey League (ESCHL) against several national powerhouse teams such as Penn State, Rhode Island, and Delaware.

Navy's hockey players, coaches, and fans yearn to rise to the challenge of playing at the NCAA Division I level, where the

University of New Hampshire, for example, plays in Hockey East. This achievement would bring with it the satisfaction of competing against the U.S. Air Force Academy at Colorado Springs and, particularly, the U.S. Military Academy at West Point, which in 2004 completed a century of collegiate hockey competition. Though academy officials and the Naval Academy Athletic Association have thus far decided to forgo a move to Division I, the team continues to develop and expand its string of winning records.

Hope springs eternal.

Other signs bode well for the development of the academy's hockey program. In 2007, the new sixteen-million-dollar Brigade Sports Complex was completed near the school. The complex has an NCAA-sized rink and a design capability for adding a second ice sheet and expanded seating, in addition to facilities for tennis and rugby. The complex was built solely through alumni donations, most notably from the late business leader Dr. J. J. McMullen, class of 1942, a former owner of the Stanley Cup–winning New Jersey Devils.

In early 2007, the NCAA selected the U.S. Naval Academy to be the collegiate sponsor for the 2009 Frozen Four national men's hockey championship finals, to be played at the Verizon Center in Washington, D.C. Additional sponsorship comes from the Washington Sports Authority and the NHL's Washington Capitals hockey club, among others. As the sports pundits like to write, these things all augur well for the future of Navy hockey.

❖ ❖ ❖

I closed my banquet speech to the 1999 Navy team, as requested, with anecdotes about playing hockey decades earlier with primitive equipment and on uncovered, natural ice. I wanted the team and its guests to know that, the obvious evolution of the sport aside, the game I played long ago was, in its essence, the same we know and love today.

In a question-and-answer period afterward, a young player rose. Why, he asked, at three times the age of the current team members, did I continue to play in goal? Why would I come out for the wild, hard-hitting, high-speed battles that typify the annual academy alumni game?

I thought about the question for only a moment. Then I grinned. "Because I can," I replied.

American team with Czech pro team, Sparta, Prague, 2004.

6

Injuries and Entropy

*So was I once myself a swinger of birches. And so I
dream of going back to be.*
> —Robert Frost

*I*n December 2007, I had rotator-cuff surgery on my right shoulder. For almost sixty-four years, about fifty-five of them playing a variety of contact sports but principally hockey, I had stoically resisted surgical repairs except facial stitches, which in the age before helmet and mask were considered de rigueur for goaltenders. I came from the Old School, in which healing ankle, knee, hip, groin, elbow, wrist, and neck damage was just a matter of time—done alone and without complaint. The postgraduates of that school believed that the main job of doctors, and particularly of surgeons, was gently but firmly to end the older athlete's playing days.

I had sustained much physical damage through the years, including the softball injury that led to my epiphany about returning to hockey. I had had serious groin tears, a chronic goalie plight caused by throwing out a leg suddenly to stop a ricocheting puck "with eyes." Lower-back problems came from being knocked into the net and against its steel supports by a falling (or pushed) attacker. One of the worst hits I have ever received came behind the net, where I had gone to retrieve a puck. Two flying youngsters ran me down. They never saw me leave the crease. I rode so hard into the boards that for days afterward I could actually feel my ribs and diaphragm twisted away from my trunk and lower body.

Due to several pinched nerves in my neck and shoulder from that episode, the fingers on my right hand were numb for months, until the nerves regenerated.

I doctored myself through most of these problems and, for the most part, played through them as well. In the winter of 2006, however, I noticed a growing weakness in my right arm and hand—my goal stick and blocker glove side. I attributed this to some unremembered hit or hard slap shot and resolved to play through it, as always.

The weakening continued, however. I felt sharp pain in the shoulder and forearm, and after more months of play, the entire arm tended to shut down. It would go numb for a minute or more if moved rapidly upward or outward—as goalies must do in making blocker saves on high or top-shelf shots. Stymied, I relented and saw a doctor, and then a second doctor, and finally a shoulder specialist, a former West Point quarterback himself, no stranger to the ravages of contact sports.

By chance, I already knew this specialist, Dr. Patrick St. Pierre, of Nirschl Orthopedic Center in Arlington, Virginia. We had met when I tried to recruit his son, Matt—an exceptional high school athlete who played hockey like a young Jaromir Jagr—for the U.S. Naval Academy club. Matt had gone on instead to a successful college hockey career at Assumption College, in Massachusetts.

Tests showed I had significant damage in the shoulder and very little strength or function in the right arm. In an attempt to avoid surgery, I agreed to a strenuous three-month rehabilitation, and to an unusual medical directive: to play frequent hockey to loosen up forcibly what was becoming a frozen shoulder.

Although the rehab program restored much of the strength and some of the function, the doctor and I deemed it unsuccessful. Not unexpectedly, as word of my infirmity got around local hockey circles, many of the goals scored on me tended to come over my right shoulder. I had little durable strength on that side and no ability to accelerate the arm and hand to deflect a shot. I was running out of options if I wanted to stay in the game at a competitive level. The rule of the hockey jungle is survival of the fittest. And I was no longer fit.

Surgery was scheduled and went well. However, it took longer than expected to repair the rotator-cuff tear, remove arthritis that had set in, and burr down an area where bone was scraping. Three more months of rehab followed, the first month without hockey, the second with hockey but no contact, the third with full contact. By the end of the rehabilitation period, I had back most of my range and function, and had started to feel like my old self in goal.

There was one marked difference, however. Decades ago, perhaps with the Seahawks, I had developed a "trick" that I came to use whenever possible in a competitive game. One of the most challenging plays for a goalie to face is a breakaway—a one-on-zero attack by a lone enemy forward. Of these classic confrontations, for the goalie the most difficult by far is when an attackman breaks in alone from a wing. He can skate untouched across the face of the goal while looking for the goalie to follow him and offer one of several openings to score.

I have always enjoyed the breakaway, which provides the netminder's ultimate challenge. And I liked the opportunity it provided to do my "trick." As the skater crossed the crease at full speed, holding the puck and looking for a scoring spot, and at the point where I was reasonably certain I was giving him no easy openings, I would suddenly skate forward, place my paddle directly between the attacker's thighs or lower legs, and twist with full strength.

At a minimum, this savage wrenching maneuver would take down the attacker, sending him sprawling into the corner. But the desired effect—the one that often brought both my team's bench and the attacker's bench to their feet, all banging their sticks against the boards in hockey's supreme expression of approval— was that when I made the torque twist between the attacker's legs, he would be immediately inverted, followed by an uncontrolled crash into the boards. Many times after initiating this unexpected aggression, I have found myself watching skate blades going past, pointed upward, at eye level.

Think about it. Regardless of his basic nature—offensive and aggressive or defensive and passive—a goalie is bound by tradition and responsibility to an essentially passive role. His opponents decide when and where to shoot and the goalkeeper must then react, but not too early for fear of making the wrong guess. Here was something I could do that, at least momentarily, reversed the roles. And, truth be told, if an opportunity to do the trick presented itself early in a contest and succeeded, breakaways declined markedly for the rest of the game. Fear and respect are wonderful motivators. Many opponents would shoot from a distance thereafter or even from the perimeter. In addition to providing a showtime event for participants and fans, I had effectively influenced the overall strategy and flow of the game to my team's advantage. No referee ever called a penalty on me for defending the crease in this manner. Ever.

But that does not imply that it was the wisest way to play. As we learned from the surgery, I had permanently damaged myself by sending the torque of flipping a heavy player upside down with my goal paddle as a strong shock directly to my shoulder countless times over the years. Needless to say, the trick is no longer in my arsenal of goaltender's weapons.

❖ ❖ ❖

The worn and damaged shoulder, now repaired, exemplifies the more general wearing out and winding down—the entropy—of my body as I have reached my mid-sixties. This is happening to every other hockey player and indeed every other human being. It is part of the cycle of life. But it is clinically interesting to have one or more opportunities every week to mark this decline in an almost scientific way by playing in goal against men typically aged from their late teens to early thirties—and here in northern Virginia, near the melting pot of Washington, D.C., to also face the varied playing styles of Russians, Czechs, Slovaks, Scandinavians, and, of course, many Canadians.

I have learned that, despite still excellent reflexes, the true sine qua non of a goalie's skill is the ability to make saves he is unaware of or does not consciously decide to make. Your body and subconscious, deep in the game and the play, simply make these saves on their own, without the involvement of your conscious mind, because there isn't time to think. On the other hand, certain maneuvers, lateral, for example, and getting up from the ice, get more difficult every year. And where once running out of drinking water created no problem beyond acute thirst, now the absence of water will quickly force cramps in the upper thighs, the calves, and even the arches of my feet.

However, if the physical changes and gradual atrophy of the body's ability is problematical but bearable, even solvable within reason, the mental dimension poses a far greater challenge when playing in a young man's game against younger men. For a younger, well-trained, and motivated hockey player, focus and discipline, the keys to individual and team success, are so ingrained as to be natural. The drive and hunger to skate quickly, play well, hit, shoot, and score or prevent a score are deep. Unrelenting.

Not so for the older player, or at least not for this older player. A goalie should always be watching the puck when it is in play, even at the other end, even in the other net. In this way the netminder stays in the game's flow and will not be surprised or unprepared when, in a matter of seconds, the puck traverses the length of the ice and is in his end, threatening his team.

Hockey is that rare game in which offense and defense change back and forth for each team, often instantaneously, many times in a single shift. But it is difficult for older players to stay intensely focused at all times, for three twenty-minute periods or for a ninety or a 120-minute pickup game. And, of course, this inattention, even if small or infrequent, will over time affect a goalie's goals-against average (GAA). It is just a natural thing—the inattention or the taking breaks from giving full attention—but its effect can decide the outcome of a game.

Unfortunately, there is more to the slow unwinding of the mind's processes, the entropy, that occurs as one ages yet attempts to play a contact sport with young men. It has to do with desire, the hunger for result. At some point the average older player, wise to the ways of the world and reasonably content with his place and success in it, can no longer summon the strong desire needed for high achievement in sports. Getting the puck over the goal line, or preventing its getting there, once occupied every atom of our beings as we strived to achieve that result for our team and for ourselves.

No more. Inevitably, it becomes more difficult to play with younger, more driven players. Although it can be faked for a while, an obvious lack of zeal will produce the same result as a lower standard of performance: In failing to meet the team's expectation, you simply will not be asked back. The need to mask a growing indifference and the urge to play more for fun, physical conditioning, and, above all, the comradeship of the game instead of winning leads to a subtle dance. This, I believe, is why many older players finally decide to leave the game. They know they are letting down their teammates, at least now and then, and yet they no longer can summon up the compulsive need or great caring for victory. Their motivations lie elsewhere.

Or perhaps it is all just a matter of chemistry. As a man ages, the body produces decreasing amounts of testosterone, a natural component in the chemistry of competition. Testosterone enhances fearlessness and persistence. When measured in athletes after contests, testosterone is often higher in winning athletes than in the defeated. An aging athlete, like a defeated athlete, may be lacking in the chemical component needed to compete successfully.

Thus, in one way or another, our physical and mental winding down, our personal entropy, is, like all naturally selective processes, slowly leading us away from genuinely competitive hockey. Are men of seventy or even eighty still playing the game capably? Absolutely. But if you watch them, as I did recently between periods of an NHL game in Washington, D.C., they are not really playing the game any longer. They are playing *at* the game. That may be enough for some. Not, I suspect, for me.

In the past year, I have played a few games as a substitute goaltender with over-forty and over-fifty groups, games in which I am still much older than most of the other players. My vanity and presumed capability found those games unsatisfying. The skating was slow. The shots were weak. Even the thinking and playmaking appeared slow-paced. Of course, I was also comparing these players to those half their age whom I faced weekly in much faster pickup games.

Then one night in one of those senior games, I was beaten 13-4. Totally shelled. Nothing like that had happened to me even when playing against professional and semipro teams in the Czech Republic several years earlier. This shelling happened before rotator-cuff surgery and I was playing with a weakened right arm. In addition, my team was outclassed from the first face-off in energy, ideas, and teamwork—everything that mattered.

But those factors had little to do with the thirteen goals. *I* was the reason for those goals, and I knew it even as they were being scored. That night I could not find in myself sufficient reason to actively resist the usual onslaughts in the goal mouth, to find the fury to fight off the whacking and hacking when I had the puck under a pad or glove but still on the ice, to make the huge save that would motivate my teammates to raise their game and stop letting the other team dictate play all over the rink.

The will to perform was just not there, and that perplexed me. It was one of the few times in my adult life when I have ever felt genuine shame while playing a sport. The goalie once asked to accompany a select team to Prague without a backup netminder, solely on his reputation for being knocked unconscious a few times over the years, then getting up and finishing his games, could not summon up enough of the necessary qualities just to stop the puck!

I get a lot of calls to play around Washington as a substitute. On any given night, I believe I can still win for any team and against any team. But something else has now changed. At one time, when the call came in, I would have my gear loaded in my old Volvo wagon and hit the road in minutes. Now, I look at the logs burning in the fireplace and at the book I am reading. I think of challenges at work in the week ahead. More often than not, I make an excuse not to play.

The question begs. Am I whispering something to myself that, sooner or later, I am bound to hear?

Hanging up the pads.

7

HANGING UP THE PADS

No memory of having starred, atones for later disregard,
or keeps the end from being hard.
                                                    —Robert Frost

Sometime in my late fifties, I mentioned offhandedly to my
father that I hoped to keep playing goal until I reached his age—
then about eighty-five—or until death deprived me of the strange
admixture of pleasure and pain that is the routine challenge of
playing that position. A typically taciturn New England Yankee, he
let his silence respond eloquently to the absurdity of my words.

Now, years later, I am reflecting on my love for this often
misunderstood game that has evolved so enormously in some
ways, yet in others remains exactly the same over the sixty years
I have laced up skates and strapped on pads. I am also confronting
the unwelcome fact that I may be coming to the end of my active
participation in hockey.

I should like to write the expected mature words, being, after
all, a mature man. I should state that I have no regrets, that I leave
the game a better player, even a better goalkeeper.

The truth lies elsewhere.

❖ ❖ ❖

I am already filled with regrets, though the event itself lies somewhere off in the indeterminate future. I know that I cannot live
forever, or react to great shots or goalmouth plays as I did as

a young man, though, of course, I do wish for those unrealistic things. And somewhere in that wish is at least a part of the reason that I keep playing.

But I also wish for a few less unrealistic things, special moments—more late-third-period situations, for example, when, with the game on the line, a swift forward darts through the defense. Suddenly, for one more time, it is just the two of us, and the shining white ice and bright lights overhead, and hundreds of expectant eyes. Dead silence, except for the sharp sound of skate blades cutting ice, and then those two or three seconds of blinding action close in, broken into smaller freeze-frame pieces for memory's storing. An ancient cat-and-mouse game of shooter and netminder played out inside the blue paint.

But I'm getting ahead of myself.

It's difficult to say where the Closing Ceremonies should actually begin for an athlete. Much depends on the sport, much on the individual. In professional sports involving contact, violence, and the expectation of high performance, most athletes leave the sport before they turn thirty, many because of lower-body injuries. Professionals fortunate enough to play into their thirties usually find that their bodies will not allow them to remain competitive through that decade. They retire with dignity and reputation intact. Every sport has notable exceptions, of course. George Blanda was kicking field goals in his fifties. "Mr. Hockey," Gordie Howe, was a superb physical specimen well into his fifties and stayed active in professional hockey, playing on a line with his two sons.

But for every George Blanda or Gordie Howe, a thousand other football or hockey professionals hung up their cleats or blades at half those ages because their bodies could not withstand another knee or hip or shoulder surgery and still perform at the required level.

We amateurs, of course, live in a world completely different from that of professionals, at least at first glance. We earn our living elsewhere. We play for the love of the game, for exercise, and for comradeship. Despite our meandering, yeomanlike efforts, we are never remotely as well conditioned as are the professionals and so, in trying to emulate them, and with our zeal and pride and love of the game, we probably expose ourselves much more to injury. That is why it is somewhat rare in contact sports like football and lacrosse and rugby, even soccer, to find many leagues of "over-thirty," "over-forty," or "over-fifty" players. The ankles, the knees, the hips, the back, the elbows, the shoulders—*and* the wives—simply cannot endure the punishment and its crippling aftermath any longer.

Despite the hard ice, solid boards and glass, and iron goal pipes, hockey is actually kinder to older bodies. When a player falls, the frictionless ice offers protection, as do modern equipment and the no-checking, no–slap shot leagues that are standard fare for older players, typically forty and above. Today across America and Canada are hundreds of teams of over forty, over fifty, over sixty, and even over seventy who play regularly and engage in tournaments as well.

But aging in a sport like hockey can pose a peculiar problem, particularly when combined with any goalie's not inconsiderable ego.

In my forties, I generally ignored my age, playing well in A and B league games against strong, young competition. The last thing on my mind was to start playing with the "old men," though some of them were younger than I. Most of the teams I played on had players grouped in the twenty-five to thirty-two age range. A few "older guys," usually defensemen, might be thirty-four to thirty-six. You could see they were slower than the norm. Often I was the only one in the locker room with gray hair and a thickening waistline.

I loved playing with those younger competitive teams, a ton of energy every night. Winning never came easily. Though we lost our share of games, I could always count on a lot of work in the crease and a ringside seat to superb hockey action. Several times in each game, those unique, point-blank moments of truth would suddenly occur that a goalie both fears and loves—fears because they strip him naked as a goaltender, loves because they give him the chance to reveal the greatness in his heart.

Somewhere in my head, I knew that I was lucky, not only to be playing, but also to be playing with and against such talented youngsters. I tried not to think about it too much, dimly aware of how fragile is a hockey goaltender's psyche and how closely the psyche is tied to his playing ability. Still, after my forty-ninth birthday, a malaise settled in.

Could a fifty-year-old goaltender still measure up, game after game, in the tough A leagues of Washington, D.C.? These were teams filled with great ex-college, ex-junior, and foreign embassy players who hadn't made the pros but who, on any given night, didn't look more than a notch or three below the NHL. The question hung above my crease throughout the fall season as our team lost two key players to injury but kept winning. Then, in a macabre solution that might have been written two thousand years earlier in a Greek tragedy, the question answered itself. I was injured in the aforementioned softball game. Though that injury is now many years and several hundred hockey games in my past, it introduced me to an athlete's physical vulnerability and my own mortality.

❖   ❖   ❖

There is a certain moment on the ice in a hockey game. The other team has scored, its members are celebrating. That insulting red goal light rotates brightly. The goalie rises from his knees or stomach or back, or from inside the net—wherever he finds himself. His final defensive actions proved insufficient. He looks at the approaching defenseman coming to retrieve the puck from the net. Their eyes lock. Volumes are spoken but usually no words.

If the defenseman came late out of the corner or did not physically counter the strong play of an attacking forward near the crease, the goalie's eyes will narrow slightly at the defenseman. The defenseman's eyes will lower, acknowledging his shortcoming. However, if the game was on the line and the shooting lanes from the point were clear, and no deflections or re-directions occurred, the goaltender's "softie" or giveaway score will draw the kind of withering look from the defenseman that one might ascribe to pity. The goalie will turn his glance away or down in shame as the defenseman removes the offending puck from the net to give to the referee.

Every goalie and every defenseman gets his share of such looks. The speed of the game and the wild caroms of the puck ensure that all players demonstrate imperfection in their play. Knowledgeable hockey players pity the players—and there are many at every level—who in the defensive zone always seem to be learning defensive responsibility, even long into otherwise distinguished hockey careers.

But were a diligent goalkeeper, amateur or professional, to plot a graph of defenseman's looks per game or week or month, he would have as good an indication as possible of the truest arc of his career. A trend toward the endgame.

I have grown tired of seeing those looks.

In my fifties, playing hockey was one long acknowledgment—a more apt word might be *lesson*—that water seeks its level. First, I learned I could no longer win consistently at the A league level. Later, I learned I could not really even play well at that level, win or lose. Either the game had sped up or I had slowed down. I could no longer carry a team at that level. This was a rude awakening.

So I became a B league substitute goalie, and won most games. I also performed well in pickup and senior select games. Just as importantly, I finally admitted to myself that I enjoyed watching an NHL or college hockey game on television at times more than I did sweating away in a goal crease at some rink for sixty minutes while twenty-something snipers tried to crack my mask and helmet with headhunter slap shots. Not surprisingly, I did not miss getting "the look" from defensemen for soft goals, either!

This was a watershed. My once extreme motivation to play and compete was falling prey to my need for comfort, for inaction, for a surrender to ambivalence. At the same time, and even as I slid further into this serenity, my great love for the game persisted, as did a nagging desire that I remain an active part of it.

I have given this thought and come to terms with its implications, as much as hockey goalkeepers ever do come to terms with a business that, in essence, asks them to stand on the ice in front of a net attired in equipment right out of the Crusades while men skating at highway speeds shoot a frozen-hard rubber disk at them with a stick. Seen in that peculiar light, can anything any goalie says or writes have a connection to the rational?

Even while fighting off or ignoring the usual middle-age-male maladies, the lingering effects of an aircraft crash at sea when a young Navy pilot, and the physical deterioration that must be expected from five decades in a hockey goal crease, I have realized this: It is not the physical but rather the mental dimension that, as we grow older, inevitably inhibits our willingness to perform at the highest levels.

This is not to say that the synapses snap as fast as they did when I was thirty. Certainly they do not. But in regularly playing in net in my sixties against teenage or twenty-something goalies, I see little difference in the reaction time of pad, stick, blocker, or glove between us. I do see the physical difference in mobility and movement, particularly side to side and up and down, due largely to weight differences and conditioning in favor of the younger netminder. But the question of patience—often the decisive goalie skill—is answered in my favor, due to age and experience.

Although my love for the game has probably deepened, the actual passion for playing it has begun to dim. And winning has definitely lost its luster. The young goaltender's almost stricken feeling when scored upon has slowly given way, first to anger or frustration, then to resistance, and then to something akin to indifference.

Many pickup games have excellent individual players, but, of course, no coaches, no game plan, and no referees. In the resulting ninety-minute, overdrive workout for goalies, each team's players concentrate their efforts at the offensive end and give little attention to defense or even the neutral zone, where real hockey games tend to be won—or lost. Is pickup hockey really hockey? I often ponder that question.

But rather than answer, I have developed a simple set of survival rules for pickup hockey that seem equitable to all. If my team is hopelessly overmatched from the first face-off, I will give an honest accounting in goal but will not pretend to be an NHL starter and try to steal the game. Not in my sixties. The outcome is presumably already known. Our play will determine only the final score.

If my team is competitive with the other team but feckless, I will encourage teammates with my play and my words, but will not try to save them from themselves. There are many children posing as adults playing amateur hockey.

But if a team, even a somewhat overmatched team, goes out on the ice and gives its heart and soul to the game, it will always get mine.

I can never be an NHL star but there are days and nights when, unbidden, my leg pads and glove and blocker make impossible saves I never see nor conceive nor react to. After those moments, I allow myself to ruminate on what life would have been like had I grown up in Canada, where my grandparents were born. I would have started skating earlier, and perhaps had the good fortune to make it to the Big Game and faced the ultimate test of skill. Hubris, of course, speaking here.

When I turned sixty, I was honored—most honored, really—to be invited to join a somewhat younger group of hockey players who were traveling to Prague, Czech Republic, to play three games against Czech teams composed of allegedly retired players. Previously my American team had journeyed to Iceland for a similar experience. I assumed I was to be the backup goalie. Au contraire, I was told.

They wanted me as the starter. They knew by reputation that even when I got knocked out, I would get back up, skate around the rink once or twice, and finish the game. Extremely handy to have your goalie possess such a "skill" when you are playing four thousand miles from home. But there was more. Because they also wanted to take along an extra defenseman, they were hoping I would not mind if the team carried just a single goalie.

Our travel arrangements worked well. The players were a skilled and amiable lot. But something was lost in the English–Czech translation. Critically, the word *retired* had not made it across the Atlantic. Upon arriving in Prague, we learned that over a four-day period we would play three opponents: the Czech Army, with several ex-NHL players; Sparta, a Czech professional team, with four players from the recent World Cup championship team; and, almost apologetically, a semipro team.

Perhaps it would be best to summarize. The Americans gave an excellent accounting of themselves, considering the opposition and the huge, unfamiliar, Olympic-sized ice sheets—and the fact that we traveled with only nine skaters and a goalie. Our final record was 0-3. Average shots per game: about seventy-five. Good-will: maximum. Fatalities: none.

For the sixty-year-old in the American net, the utter impossibility of each of those 180 minutes throughout those three games proved a gripping lifetime experience. I experienced a thrill to represent my country in some small and unofficial way, in a sport played at a very high level by teams from another nation. It was obvious during the warm-ups who would win each game. But playing for personal vanity or pride and even for our team's reputation was not enough. Something like national dignity required that we play well enough against those heavy odds—ten of us against twenty-two of them, younger, bigger, and much better. That we hold our own. We had to fashion our own form of victory, not on the scoreboard, which was not possible, but in the skirmishes, in the face-offs, and in the goalmouth scrambles. Finally, when each game ended, those great Czech players needed to know that they had been tested in a hockey game. And that was exactly how it played out.

❖ ❖ ❖

How does this story turn out?

Part of me hopes I can keep on going indefinitely. But when I say such nonsense to my father, now over ninety-one years old, his silence, like Sir Thomas More's, betokens much. I read the wisdom in his eyes, just as he reads the disappointment in mine, at the news he does not have to give me but that we both inherently know.

At some point, everything must end. The evidence, as they say, is compelling.

❖ ❖ ❖

Not one year ago, I played at least two games each week. Now I am fortunate to play one. Whether or not the excuses are legitimate, I may go two or three weeks without playing. This leaves me wearing unfamiliar equipment and performing a challenging function that feels awkward. To come back from a layoff, it is always good to have a key victory or at least a good personal performance to build upon. I do not always have those anymore. Most of my recent performances have been forgettable. A few hockey-playing friends have asked if I am healthy. What do I reply? I am, at least physically.

Of course, all goalies, even the pros, go through up-and-down cycles, both mental and physical. I recently substituted in a seniors game and for the first time in years was beaten in double figures. That the defense was pitiful was beside the point. In that game I found that my old reliable rage, which I have always called upon to direct against the opposition, referees, teammates, even myself, failed utterly to materialize in the face of an aggressive team bearing down on my lackluster mates. It had evaporated. Other than squaring up on the shooters and playing the puck, I did not have it in me to try to be a goalie and two defensemen at the same time. The question: Have I grown to a new level of wisdom in the game or am I merely a worn-out old netminder who doesn't know when to quit?

❖ ❖ ❖

Answer: It is a month later, deep in winter. I am visiting frigidly cold seacoast New Hampshire to check on my father. As always, my goalie skates are with me. A member of Rye's Hockey Remnant, the last hockey-playing group in this one-time bastion of the sport, calls to say they are playing a pickup game on the golf course pond Sunday morning at nine, shoveling to begin at eight.

I go. In the garage hang a battered pair of Vaughn goal pads and an old CCM goalie paddle made of papier-mâché held together with tape. We shovel. Then we ring the cleared playing area with long four-by-fours. Then we play. For two hours.

Indoor, lighted, artificial rinks and warm dressing rooms make it easy to forget the pond hockey of one's boyhood, sitting on the bank, butts freezing, the race to get skates laced before fingers go numb. Similarly forgotten is the simple beauty of shinny itself—deft stick handling; crisp, accurate passing; snap shots into a scrap lumber goal or just between a pair of L.L. Bean boots.

I have never seen the sky a deeper blue than on that day. The snow-covered spruce trees lining the banks of the pond help break some of the Montreal Express wind. But five degrees is five degrees—until, that is, the game gets going.

With the old pads, goal skates, a goal stick I could have broken apart with my bare hands, a leather bomber jacket, driving gloves, and a Navy watch cap drawn low over my eyebrows for "protection," despite the gratuitous no-lifting rules that I have seen ignored a thousand times on Rye ice, I lived in goalie heaven for two blessed hours that day, stopping dozens of shots from old friends, a former Rye Seahawk among them. Only two goals are scored—one on a clean breakaway where I made a bad guess, the other a skate deflection in front on a third rebound shot. Do I want either back? Nope. Can I play better than that? Nope!

Were someone at that moment to have decided that my time on earth was to come to an end and called me home right there from the ice, I could only have said with my final breath: What better place? What better time? What better game?

❖ ❖ ❖

I do not know what the future holds for my now tenuous connection to the game of hockey. What player does? Last year here in Washington, D.C., in an amateur league game, another goaltender, a fifty-one-year-old firefighter, was playing and failed to get up after a scramble in the crease. He was pronounced dead of a heart attack. We all mourn his loss. None of us know when our time will come.

One night a few years ago, I had the occasion to play back-to-back league games. I completed one game for my regular team. Then another team's goalie did not show up and I was asked to step in. Both were fast, competitive games with a lot of work in goal. Lots of rubber. After the second game, I had to rest awhile and rehydrate before finding the strength to remove upper-body armor and goal pads.

As I sat there, a player I did not know sat down to thank me for filling in. Then, I suspect to lessen the burdens he felt I might be experiencing due to age or exhaustion, he told me there was an eighty-four-year-old goaltender playing regularly in the senior league at that rink. Everyone loved to watch him, he said. With his old knees, he could no longer go down to the ice. But he was wise in the ways of the game—always square to the shooter, good with stick and glove, and therefore pretty hard to score on. At age eighty-four! Feeling twenty years younger, I thanked the young player for his kindness, jumped up, and began to quickly peel off my equipment as if I was going to a fire. Me, old? I suddenly felt like a new man. A *young* man!

But reality always returns. I know that my body will not allow me to play as much in the future. I hope, however, to continue playing regularly enough that I will not begin to lose the basic skills and instincts needed to perform at what may be the most difficult and challenging position in any sport.

For more than five decades, the game of hockey and the unique challenges of goaltending have formed one of the primary interests and deepest currents of my life, enhancing it and enriching it. I can scarcely imagine having lived my life without hockey—without, strange as it may sound, stopping those now countless pucks.

The true measure of how deeply love for this game can be found in the chambers of my heart will likely be found on the white ice of Alexandria, Virginia's indoor rinks and the black ice of Rye, New Hampshire's ponds, some twenty or more years from now. If I am still at that time given the gift of this game, I will count myself among the fortunate few so blessed. That I will one day hang up the pads is, of course, beyond question. But the day and the date remain unknown.

Until then, just keep those pucks coming!

8

THE RYE REMNANT

But still unstoried, artless, unenhanced, such as she was; such as she would become.

—Robert Frost

What is a hockey town?

Whatever it is, there are hundreds of them in New England loyal to the Boston Bruins or to their AHL, college, or high school team, but mostly to the sport itself. They love the teamwork, speed, precision, courage, even the violence, and the great competitive heart of man so obvious in the colorful combat on cold, unforgiving ice.

In the mid-1940s, as the great cataclysm called World War II ended, the seacoast New Hampshire town of Rye was transformed into a genuine hockey town. There, in a village of just over a thousand souls, a group of former school chums turned battle-hardened war veterans found fellowship playing hockey on the town's ponds.

One thing led to another. A vacant lot was bulldozed flat. Rough lumber "borrowed" from an old National Guard encampment site became side boards, trees were trimmed into light poles, equipment was donated, and a team was born. For a decade the Rye Seahawks knew fame across northern New England playing other teams of war veterans. They gave as good as they got in contests among players who probably saw hockey as a clambake after years of serious labor on the front lines of Europe or the Pacific.

Each winter the townspeople turned out regularly to cheer on their team. Most sat in their cars, motors running, heaters on, for winters were much colder then. But many did not have cars, which had not been produced since the beginning of the war. Some, in fact, did not have jobs.

The days of indoor covered rinks, artificial brine ice, and Zamboni ice-cleaning machines were still a twinkle in some visionary's eye. The Seahawks played through years of bitter cold spells and great winter storms. It was common practice for the Rye team to go to the rink the morning after a heavy storm, shovel off a foot or more of snow, flood the ice with a thin layer of water from a nearby fire hydrant, then head to their jobs. After supper that evening, team members returned to the rink, put on their equipment in their cars or outside on a bench, then played a game against a visiting team from places like Amesbury, Laconia, and Biddeford. When the game concluded, the players would again scrape the ice with shovels and hand plows, then lay out hose from the fire hydrant and flood the surface to provide a smooth sheet for the next day.

It was a beautiful moment in time, the 1946–1960 reign of the Rye Seahawks, with the town's strong support for the team. And of something deeper: The sense of identifying with the team's fortunes, its victories and defeats, was palpable in the community as well.

But the veterans were getting into their thirties as the 1940s gave way to the 1950s, and their legs were getting heavier. New blood was brought to the team, including a handful of us barely into high school. The result did not match up well against teams Rye traditionally played from New Hampshire, Maine, and Massachusetts. Victories became rarer, defeats were the norm. By 1960, the team ceased play forever.

I was thinking of that long-ago era when visiting my parents in Rye a few years back. Because of the Seahawks' strong influence on the town's youth, on any winter afternoon, and seemingly all weekends, hockey games took place on every pond in town. The little kids on their "double-runners" played in some protected corner with mothers close by. Grade schoolers emulated their elders in what passed for a hockey game. But at the center of the pond, with admiring groups of girls in bright hats, mittens, and sweaters clumped about, and piles of boots, jackets, and spare sticks here and there, one would find the featured game of teenagers and young adults—the Seahawks wannabes. This was real end-to-end hockey, with all the shouting and striving, sounds of stick on stick and skates cutting ice, yells of jubilation and sighs of despair.

Where had it all gone? I drove down Love Lane past Browns Pond, then down Central Road past Burkes Pond near the Abenaqui Golf Course. The Abenaqui's water hazards often doubled handily as rinks in winter. Not a single skater glided on the beautiful broad expanses of black ice. Black ice was the skater's and hockey player's dream, excepting goalkeepers. Goalies sometimes had difficulty sorting out a black puck from black ice on such a pond.

Where was everybody? Did folks skate only indoors these days? I thought about that for a minute. The closest indoor ice was in Exeter, almost half an hour away. Would people make that drive just to avoid a little cold and wind? Apparently so.

But what of all the other things lost, important things? What of the solitary skating adventures along streams, practicing stick-and-puck and power skating and spying fish and turtles through the ice at the same time? What of meeting neighborhood friends to play early-morning hockey on a pond in the woods? What of hot chocolate from a plaid thermos and a peanut butter and jelly sandwich wrapped in wax paper as your lunch? What of all-day, father-and-son hockey games on the frozen freshwater expanse of Eel Pond?

Eel Pond. I had forgotten about that half-mile-long pond, home to muskrats and red-winged blackbirds, surrounded by craggy granite ledge. Hoping against hope, I turned down Sea Road, then north on the Route 1A shore road toward the harbor.

And there they were, far off in the southwest corner of the great pond, where the ice was perhaps smoothest or the treed shoreline offered some protection from the wind. A group of bright hockey jerseys, predominantly red or blue, moved back and forth, cutting, weaving, and waving sticks for passes. No sound traversed the distance. The scene was silent.

The day brightened. Hockey lived on in Rye. If only a reminder from the glory days, it *was* a hockey game. A remnant—the Rye Remnant—of the town's great hockey past still played.

❖ ❖ ❖

I parked the car, zipped up my coat, pulling my hat down well over my ears, and got out. Living in Virginia, I had forgotten the acute cold of a New England winter, the cutting chill of its wind. But the familiar activity out on the ice, evoking memories of hundreds of days spent skating on this and other Rye ponds, hastened my adjustment. I trudged across the pond's icy surface.

Within minutes I could hear the crack of stick on stick, the shouts of players involved in the sweep of the game. The play was of high caliber. Passes were crisp, stick handling deft, skating fast, and on-ice decisions faster: pond hockey at its best.

I approached to a shouted greeting, then to a challenge to defend one of the goals! Once a goaltender, always . . . I had left several front teeth and an eyebrow on a rink just up the road forty years earlier in those days before helmets and masks. I had no strong desire now to explain to my family how in middle age, I managed to forgo all wisdom and repeat those injuries, incurring new scars.

But some things are just meant to happen. And at times the daft receive protection from above. Soon I was drawn into that happiest of sports experiences—pond hockey played fast on good ice by players who love the game, on a beautiful sunny day with a dark blue sky and ice like glass.

❖ ❖ ❖

That day led to other, similar days. And then to something of a tradition. Once or twice a year, usually in December or January, I receive a midweek call from one of the remnant players inviting my participation in full goaltending gear for the following weekend, when weather conditions should be ideal. Translation? Frigid!

Somewhere, in a backyard junk jumble or perhaps in the old town icehouse, someone finds a rusty regulation goal, nets hanging askew, and trucks it to the designated pond.

There, for at least one weekend, players accustomed to a goalie-less game get to take out all of their scoring hunger on a figure in the crease who is at least dressed for the part. The first year I brought the gear, my parents came down to watch (and perhaps to pray). I was taking warm-up shots in goal when a late arrival pulled up, hopped out of his pickup, grabbed skates and sticks, and headed through the trees toward the ice. Suddenly he stopped short, seeing the novelty of goal and goalie for the first time, and loudly exclaimed, "Oh, boy, we have a goalie!"—words well understood by every hockey player on earth.

❖ ❖ ❖

Like all hockey events, the Remnants' weekend games have long had their traditions and rituals. Anyone could come and play but the speed and finesse of the game subtly discouraged the return of "pylons," players who could not keep up with the flow or make a contribution. Over the years, many of the faces have changed but many have stayed the same.

Before play begins, the players scrape the ice clean with shovels. Then four-by-fours are placed to form a boundary to contain the puck. A red line is poured from a gallon jug of bug juice. Two-by-four goals with capped ends are positioned at each end. Other than skates and sticks and a hockey sweater, few players wear protective equipment such as gloves, shin guards, or helmets. Injuries are rare, but accidents do happen in a game played with such high energy and great speed.

The idea of dressing out a goaltender, however, is to give players a chance to try shots, particularly the kind that their "no-lifting" rules would not regularly allow. In warm-ups, with no unprotected players in the way, some will also want to see how much moxie they can still coax out of their slap shots. One difference from the indoor rink is the hundred-foot walk through snow on skates to retrieve a wild shot. One or two long strolls usually discourage the practice.

Over nearly twenty years since I rediscovered hockey on Eel Pond, and have occasionally joined this remnant of Rye's glory years as a genuine hockey town, I have experienced some wonderful moments. The players include one former Seahawk, sons of Seahawks, even grandsons of Seahawks.

We often played in weather so cold that it was a race to get skates laced and pads strapped on before fingers lost the capability to function. A water bottle once froze solid atop my goal in a matter of minutes. The wind sometimes blew so fiercely at my back that every time a breakout began from the other end and I turned to check my position relative to the goal, I'd find it fifteen or twenty feet behind me.

❖ ❖ ❖

As with everything in life, hockey is mostly about people. After five decades in a hockey goal, I now see that while the game's excitement and passion and competition lure me back onto the ice, the deeper satisfactions come from loving the game and those who play it. I know, *love* is a strange word coming from a hockey player. But it is true. Love of each other, teammate and opponent, and of the game itself. I witness this love in every game I play.

It is a Sunday game on an Abenaqui Pond, off Fairway Drive. The pressure is on at our end of the ice. Lots of shots. Too many rebounds. Finally we gain control and start our breakout. The Carberry brothers, Michael and Tim, skate deftly forward. I've known them since they were five-year-old hecklers behind the end boards and chicken wire and I was the Seahawks teenage goaltender in 1958 and 1959. Their father, a paper route customer, taught me everything I ever learned about rebuilding old cars.

I relax and straighten up from my goalie crouch. Suddenly, Tim turns with the puck, looks at me, and in a blink uncorks a wicked slap shot that, caught unawares, I just barely snag near the upper corner of the net. "What the hell?" I sputter. "You're *my* defenseman!"

Tim smiles back broadly. "You just looked like you were lonely and needed that shot to stay awake back there," he said.

Rye hockey. . . .

Another cold day on Burkes Pond and I'm in goal in a great end-to-end game. Suddenly, I have a déjà-vu moment. I watch the center man on the opposing side break out from behind his own goal and speed up ice toward me. Something about the wide strides of his skating style looks familiar. The blond head and stick handling as well. I am instantly taken back to a Seahawks scrimmage fifty years earlier, the same skater coming straight at me centering the town team's first line. It is shifty center Phil Drake. I can hardly bear the realization that this skater in the present is Phil's son, Frank. A spitting image. Unbidden, tears well up. I feel ancient. What am I doing in this equipment? Why am I here, attempting to play goal against the son of my teammate from fifty years ago? There is something almost gloriously painful in the idea, and I stifle a sob. Unseemly for a hockey player—tears.

As if to bring me back to reality, Frank head-fakes a back-checking center, breaks to his left, then neatly feathers a saucer pass onto the stick of his lanky right wing as he accelerates over the bug-juice red line. *CRACK!* The sound of the slap shot occurs almost simultaneously with the arrival of the blunt-force impact of the rising hard shot striking the armor near my clavicle. It ricochets high into the air and flies off into the snow. The young shooter grins as he heads to retrieve the puck. I realize he is the graduate student son of still another former Seahawk, my old friend John Clifford, who is also in the game. I feel yet another rush of deep feeling, emotion and memory. How quickly these generations come and go. It is not easy to see those pucks through tears.

❖ ❖ ❖

Another game, another year. The devil himself plays among us, at least that is how I am seeing it from behind my goalie's mask. Mark Webb, once a local and now living in the South, who looks like a teenager but admits to being "around forty," is a man of contradictions. But there is nothing contradictory about his hockey skills. A Gretzky look-alike, his skates are more dangerous near the crease than are the sticks of many other players. Mark is blessed with immense natural skill—great eyesight, balance, and coordination. Unknowingly, he will create pure magic on the ice. At times he effortlessly moves the puck through a scrum of players, approaching the goal, and, half a dozen fakes, dekes, and misdirection moves later, the puck is . . . well, you know where it is.

One recent winter Mark and I found ourselves on the black ice of Eel Pond on a gray, overcast day skating just for exercise. One thing led to another. I put on my goalie pads and gloves and mask but no other equipment. Using as the goal a rocky outcropping on the shoreline, the two of us commenced about an hour or so of cat-and-mouse exchanges, shooter and goaltender. The shooter, breaking in, tries various speeds and techniques to beat the goalie, shooting or sliding the puck past him. The goalie, looking for the poke check, exhibits patience, showing no openings, staying on his skates as long as possible trying to defeat the attack. A hockey ballet for two.

Later, we skated back across the huge pond to our cars, arguing all the way where and how the shooter or the goalie could best find advantage in this age-old contest. As we left the granite outcropping, I noticed that we had skated a perfect circle of white on the black ice where we had battled to settle the ancient issue, and hadn't. But—Tabernac!—the joy of trying!

The oldest of the Rye Remnant, and the last Seahawk regularly skating, is John Clifford. A retired dentist, he is the senior skater, the gray eminence on the pond. John has me by about a year. We have compared notes and believe we have played hockey together since 1952. Fifty-six years. And it might have been a year or two before that.

John and I grew up in a fortunate era when children seemed to have total freedom, and they used that freedom to play sports or for other independent outdoor activity every waking minute they weren't in school or doing homework. Homework?

Boys growing up in Rye had one other advantage. We had dozens of athletic family men in town to play with and receive instruction from in sports. We also played against the friars of Saint Francis Friary in Rye Beach, a landmark now long gone. Those men gave us extraordinary lessons in sports, in sportsmanship, and in life. We stubbornly battled them in basketball and hockey, rarely winning but attaining knowledge and skill in the games from their high level of play. I wonder where our young get such support today.

John Clifford and I were two of the four high schoolers brought up to the Seahawks in the late 1950s to fill the thinning ranks of original World War II veterans. Two years after John and I joined, the Rye hockey team was history.

John, all sinew then as he is now, was the classic center man—fast, shifty, patient with the puck, and an excellent shooter. As a youngster, he carried about him the aura of everyone's concern because he had an enlarged heart. It is a concern now obviously laid to rest by his half century as an active sportsman.

John was the only boy I knew with sufficient drive to save his summer-job money and buy the best-quality CCM skates—Super Tacks—at a time when few but the pros wore professional skates. But if you'd seen him then, skating against teams of men twice his age, you could understand why he wanted this advantage and also how well he employed it.

John's long skating stride never changed but now, well past sixty, he picks his active spots in the game. In one weekend scrimmage a few years ago, however, I began to wonder whether John was hurt or, worse, if his days on the ice were nearing an end. His skating was less fluid. Several younger players burned him going the other way. He seemed to be playing more passively and on the periphery of the game. Behind the goalkeeper's mask, one sees everything.

Suddenly, as if he'd heard me and was somehow goaded by my unintended insult, John faked a shot from the left point, moved swiftly outside his man, and broke toward the net. A defender moved to check him. John head-faked inside and the younger player, taking the fake, turned toward the middle. John—not the assumed geriatric I had just been worrying about but someone from decades earlier—sped toward the near goal post untouched.

I hugged the post, crouched low, and prepared for the contest. John slowed as he crossed the crease, looking to the near top corner. I stayed on my feet, giving away nothing. He ducked his head and kept motoring parallel to the goal line. I moved with him and partially opened the five hole invitingly, like a pretty girl lifting her hem slightly when looking for a ride. He looked, read and rejected my ruse, and moved on. I gambled and stayed on my feet, hoping for defensive help. None came. By now John was at the right side of the crease and starting to open slightly on the goal. It was the moment of truth. I sprawled to my knees, at the same time elevating my upper body and arms as much as possible to defend the top shelf. Too late. With a classic sniper's move, John's stick beat my skate to the right post and put the puck into the net.

I looked up and saw the twinkle in John's eye as he skated up ice to rejoin brothers Tommy and Billy for the next rush, and I thought to myself, "That Seahawk will be playing the game for quite a few more years."

❖   ❖   ❖

Perhaps what we have here is no magical happening or great tradition, but instead a group of folks who have simply lost their minds. Why, when you can hop in your car and drive a civilized half hour to an indoor rink, dress out in cozy warmth, and play hockey in predictable weather conditions on perfect ice, would we shovel and build a rink, risking frost bite and possible immersion to play outdoors?

Fair question.

Answer: Because it's there. Because it's free. Because it's ours.

It is each of these things, of course, and much more. Natural ice, and particularly great expanses of natural ice, and most particularly great expanses of natural black ice, have an unfathomable allure for hockey players. Black ice presents at once an object of beauty, a territory to be explored, and a means of vigorous exercise. It is available only seasonally in certain places. For those who choose to live in a cold region, black ice symbolizes where we live and who we are. And more. Everything worthwhile requires effort and sacrifice, even pain. If an easier or warmer life were wanted, there are many other places to live. Places with no winter to speak of. And no ice to skate on. And what kind of life would that be?

The Rye Remnant does not have to exist. Nobody is required to play hockey on Rye ponds each winter's Saturday and Sunday morning, weather and ice permitting, from nine to eleven AM. But the Remnant does. Among the players are former team members, their sons, grandsons, and other relatives, of a Rye town hockey team that played its final game in the year 1960. Names like Drake, Peyser, Clifford, and Carberry, who are playing today, may be found in team records from the 1940s and 1950s.

Is there a hidden or higher meaning, something an anthropologist would discern a thousand years hence? I think so. A hockey town is a hockey town is a hockey town, even in the age of the Internet and HDTV, the iPod and Nintendo. Fundamental things in nature do not change. Rye will always be a hockey town. Without offering anyone a million-dollar contract—or any contract at all—the game has been remarkably preserved at a high level of skill, almost as if in amber, by the Rye Remnant. By John, Tommy, and Billy Clifford; Frank Drake; Rick Peyser; Michael, Tim, and Michelle Carberry; Dave Duquenne; Peter Cady; Jeff Knapp; George Bushway; Mark Webb—occasionally, Bruce Valley—and others from Rye.

❖ ❖ ❖

How does it all play out, far off in the misty future? I can see it in my crystal ball. Years or even decades from now, some of the children of Rye grow bored with their remarkable electronic toys and gizmos and personal spacecraft. They seek out simple, more earthly interests. They rediscover, of all things, their beautiful town—its craggy granite coastline, its verdant woods, its ponds and estuaries. In winter, fatigued by information and electronic overload, they don skates found in dusty attics to explore the frozen expanses of the town's many ponds. And at one of them—lo—they spy bright red and blue jerseys surging to and fro, see sticks raised and clashing, hear shouts of rage and joy.

What is this? they ask. How very interesting. A game? How fast it goes. *Can we play?* And with that question, a chortle is heard in the clouds above and the Town of Rye enters another renaissance as a hockey town. And those many of us who so love the game and play no longer will rest more easily at hearing the sounds of shouting, skates cutting ice, and stick on puck as yet another generation of Rye youngsters feels the adrenaline rushing up ice while playing the world's greatest game.

The Rye Seahawks cast long shadows.

Eel pond vintage hockey tableau. (© Peter E. Randall)

Appendix A

ROSTERS OF SEAHAWKS PLAYERS

1940s

Lee Berry D
Ralph Berry F
Dave Boise D
John Carberry F
Harlan Carter D
John Carter F
Frankie Ciolek F
Dick Corso F
John "Peanut" Culliton D
Phil Drake F
Henry Duchesne F
Dan "Dinny" Fogerty F
Phil Goss F
Jack Hayes F
Ed Herlihy F
Sonny Higgins F
Winn Hoyt D
Bill Jenness D
Irving "Flash" Jenness D
Guy Kelsey G/D
Dick Locke G
Bill Lorenz D
Bob Lovett D
Gene/William Merrill F
Pete Meyer G
Jim Morrison F
Bill Moulton D
Robert Pearson D
Dick Peyser F
Leighton Remick D
Phil Reynolds F
Ralph Sargent D
Bob "Sully" Sullivan G
Bill White D
Dick Wilson F
Stu Wright F

1950s

Joe Belmont F
Dave Bunting F
Frank Capone F
John Clifford F
Dick Daley D
Doug Gaskell F
Gordie Gaskell D
Lenny Goyette D
Bill Hamilton D
Barney Laughlin G
Dick Lilly D
Dr. Rolf Lium
Bud Loosemore D
Dave Meehan F
Jim Morrison D
Bobby Oeser F
Jimmy Oeser F
Rick Oeser D
Anse Palmer D
Jim Philbrick F
Ned Pointer D
Center Sanders D
JC Sanders F
Ronnie Sleeth F
Melvin Trefethen D
Bruce Valley G

Position:
Forward (F)
Defense (D)
Goal (G)

87

Appendix B

SEAHAWKS OPPONENTS

Laconia, N.H. (All-Stars
Wolfboro, N.H. (Abenaqui Indians
Manchester, N.H. (St. Jean's)
Manchester, N.H. (St. Anselm's
Dover, N.H. (American Legion)
Dover, N.H. (Mohawks)
Portsmouth, N.H. (VFW)
Hampton, N.H.
Berlin, N.H. (Maroons)
Nashua, N.H. (Royals)
Suncook, N.H.
Concord, N.H. (Sacred Heart)
Exeter, N.H. (Knights of Columbus)
Lewiston, Maine
Biddeford, Maine (Cyclones)
Biddeford, Maine (St. Andre's Flying Frenchmen)
Westbrook, Maine (Crusaders)
Ogunquit, Maine (Blue Fins)
Brunswick, Maine (Bowdoin College)
Saco, Maine (Silver Skates)
Weymouth, Mass. (Cubs)
Amesbury, Mass. (Maple Leafs)
Amesbury, Mass. (Indians)
Haverhill, Mass. (Ryans)
Lynnfield, Mass. (Knights)
Gloucester, Mass. (Fishermen)
Newburyport, Mass. (Don Boscos)
Newburyport, Mass. (Paramount Jewelers)
Melrose, Mass.
Winchester, Mass.
Lynn, Mass. (General Electric)
Beverly, Mass. (Flyers)
North Andover, Mass.
Danvers, Mass. (Bay Staters)
South Peabody, Mass.
Saugus, Mass.
Squantum, Mass. (Naval Air Station)
Cambridge, Mass. (Hartnett All-Stars)

Acknowledgments

No book can be written without significant assistance.

I am indebted to those who gave so much of their time recounting details of Rye's hockey team: Phil Drake, Leighton Remick, Jack Hayes, Priscilla Jenness, Shirley Carter, Dave Boise, Frank Ciolek, John Culliton, Bob Lovett, John Clifford, Rick Oeser, Gordie Gaskell, Barney Laughlin, Jim Philbrick, and Dick Lilly.

Shirley Carter, Priscilla Jenness, and Frank Ciolek also loaned scrapbook holdings, which were of inestimable value to my research and to getting facts into the story.

Several people were kind enough to read an early draft of the manuscript for historical accuracy: Frank Ciolek, Jack Hayes, John Clifford, Leon Valley, and Tom and Rosemary Clarie, authors of the well-regarded *Just Rye Harbor: An Appreciation and History*. Tom Clarie's assistance was particularly valuable, as his insights brought the draft into better focus.

Many others made important contributions:

Publisher Peter Randall, long the literary lion in my life, suggested a story-line change that took an additional year but delivered the goods.

Author Dan Brown, of Rye Beach, made helpful suggestions early in the project.

Kim Crooker, my coworker, bore the burden of typing the manuscript through its many iterations.

Amy Babcock, my friend, brought experience and profession-alism to the initial editing process.

Nicole Cloutier, Special Collections librarian, Portsmouth Public Library, reviewed *Portsmouth Herald* sports stories from 1946 to 1955 on microfilm, and provided the collection of news articles about the team found in appendix C.

Leon Valley, my father, gave the Town of Rye over fifty years of service and a zoning ordinance that, purchased with a ten-dollar vote recount fee from his wallet, brought environmental stability to the town's future. He also gave me a quality no goalkeeper or writer should lack—tenacity.

Finally, Nancy Valley, my wife and the love of my life, provided the inspiration, as she has done consistently across the decades.

Thanks to each for his or her help and support on this journey.

I alone remain responsible for any incorrect statements, facts, dates, and any other errors.

Bruce Valley
9433 Forest Haven Drive
Alexandria, Virginia 22309

brucevalley@earthlink.net

Appendix C

SELECTED NEWS STORIES

PORTSMOUTH, N. H., THURSDAY EVENING, DECEMBER 23, 1948

Rye Hockey Club Cancels Tonight's Opening Game

Pucksters Seek Saturday Contest; Danvers in Sunday

Poor ice conditions have caused a cancellation of the opening of the hockey season by the Rye Hockey club.

The Rye pucksters were scheduled to open tonight against the Dover Legion but snow on the ice as well as poor freezing temperatures have nullified the attempt to break the ice on the new season.

Manager Johnny Carter said that he is trying to book a game for Saturday night with the Dover team or some other sextet which would be willing to journey to Rye for the contest.

Ice conditions in Dover are as bad as they are here so the game cannot be played in Cochecotown either.

The snow last Sunday was cleared from the Rye rink just in time for the Tuesday sprinkling. However the high temperatures caused melting and the ice on the rink is very bumpy.

THE RYE CLUB definitely will open its season Sunday night against the Danvers hockey team. Of course, ice conditions will be a major factor in this encounter but the Danvers tilt is a scheduled contest.

The Rye club has 24 games scheduled for the winter weeks and the cancelled game tonight will be pushed back until later in the season when conditions are favorable.

The rink has been moved this year and it is located right beside the road along route 1-A just north of Perkins road. Fans also may use the warming house built by the club for use during the cold winter afternoons and evenings.

Hockey Club Whips Danvers Sextet,

The Portsmouth Herald, Portsmouth, N. H.
Monday Evening, December 27, 1948

Wilson, Peyser, Ciolek Score 2

Chilling their opponents in the near zero weather, Rye Hockey club blasted its way to a 7-4 victory over Danvers Hockey club in the season's opener at the Rye Beach rink last night.

The Rye sextet apparently iced the game in the first two periods as the forward lines were very effective and Bob Sullivan turned back thrust after thrust of the Bay State invaders.

Frank Ciolek scored the first goal of the season when he rammed home a shot after taking a pass from Leighton Remick. The goal came about five minutes after play had opened. Dick Peyser dropped the second one through for the Rye club when he took a pass from Dave Boles in 10:00.

Danvers was unable to break down the six-goal lead Rye built up in the opening periods despite the fact it put on a last minute burst. The summary:

RYE	DANVERS
Sullivan, g	g, Putnam
W. Jenness, ld	rd, Smith
Boles, rd	ld, Andrus
Peyser, lw	rw, Pyndenkowsky
Carter, c	c, Chase
R. Wilson, rw	lw, A. Koban

Officials: Lorenz and Sweetser.
Rye spares—Kesley, Hayes, Page, Hoitt, W. Wilson, Ciolek, White, Remick, I. Jenness, Colliton.

Danvers spares—Leathe, G. Koban, Batchelder, Hazen, Gongas, Garron, Mitchell.

First period: Rye: Ciolek (Remick), 5:00; Peyser (Bols) 10:00.

Second period: Rye: R. Wilson (unassisted) 4:00; Carter (Peyser) 10:00; Peyser (unassisted) 12:00; Danvers: Pyndenkowsky (unassisted) 15:00; Rye: R. Wilson, (Boles) 16:00.

Third period: Danvers: Smith (Batchelder) 11:00; Danvers: Smith (Batchelder) 14:00; Rye: Ciolek (unassisted) 18:00; Danvers: Batchelder (unassisted) 19:00.

Penalties: First period — Leathe, tripping. Second period—Smith, tripping; Coburn, tripping: Colliton and Batchelder, roughing: White, charging. Third period—Remick, roughing: Gongas, extra man on ice.

Officials: Bill Lorenz and Jack Sweetser, referees. Jack Lorenz, timer.

January 31, 1949

Rye Hockey Club Drops Tournament Game, 5 - 4

Rye Hockey club missed its chance for a bid to the State hockey tournament of champions at Berlin by one goal as they dropped a 5-4 decision to St. Jean's Maple Leafs at the southern New Hampshire tourney in Manchester over the weekend.

The tournament was won by Laconia All-Stars who edged the Maple Leafs, 7-6, in the finals last night.

Laconia edged Dover's Legionnaires, 5-3, to win the semi-final game played in the afternoon while Rye dropped its close decision to the Leafs in the second game.

* * *

RYE WENT out ahead, 2-0 in the early minutes of the second game on fast breakaways by John Carter and Frank Ciolek, but the Maple Leafs got back into the game on three successive goals before the first period ended.

Sullivan tallied first for the locals at 7:22 and was followed to the net by Frank Noel, who scored unassisted at 13:51. With seconds remaining, Sullivan again tallied on a neat cage-circling maneuver in which he beat the Rye goalie unassisted, at the left corner of the cage.

From that point on, the locals were never headed, both teams tallying twice in the second period, Rye coming from behind, 5-2, to threaten on tallies by Dick Wilson, assisted by Dick Peyser at 9:49 and by Joe Belmont, assisted by Bill Jenness at 12:24.

A see-saw battle prevailed throughout the final period, featured by fast breakaways and wild melees at the cages, but neither team could score, giving the Maple Leafs the victory.

* * *

. THE LACONIA clan battered its way to a 4-1 first-period lead against the Dover sextet in the opener, with Frank Lamiere in the starring role as he tallied two goals within the first two minutes of play.

The second period, however, turned out to be a see-saw battle, with neither team scoring until the 13-minute mark, when John Gitscher tallied unassisted after a faceoff near the Laconia net.

In the third canto, Rob Poire and Dan Fogarty provided a tally for each team with Laconia getting the win on its early scoring.

This contest provided the day's only major penalty, when Lee Lamiere of Laconia was sidelined for hooking. Gitschier's penalty shot was easily blocked by Laconia's Goalie John Richardson.

St. Jean Mapleleafs	Rye Hockey C.
Plourde, lw	rw, Wilson
Sullivan, c	c, J. Carter
F. Noel, rw	lw, Peyser
Kelley, ld	rd, W. Jenness
Stillman, rd	ld, Culliton
Daragon, g	g, Sullivan

St. Jean spares: H. Noel, Allaire, Jannelle,p Bouchard, Houle, J. Martineau.

Rye spares: Remick, Belmont, Irv Jenness, Colier, Drake, H. Carter, Hoyt, W. Hayes, J. Hayes and Kelsey.

First period: Rye, J. Carter (Wilson) 1:27; Colier, unassisted 6:21; St. Jean, Sullivan, (Kelley) 7:22; F. Noel, unassisted 13:51; Sullivan, unassisted 14:58.

Second period: St. Jean, Janelle (Kelley) 2:14; Janelle (Bouchard) 6:52; Rye, Wilson (Peyser) 9:49; Merrill (Jenness) 12:24.

The Portsmouth Herald, Portsmouth, N. H.
Thursday Evening, February 3, 1949

Rye Ties Dover Legion; Newburyport in Tonight

Seventy minutes of fast hockey yielded nothing for the Rye Hockey club and the Dover Legion as the two sextets battled to a 5-5 overtime tie last night on the Dover rink.

Rye will play again tonight as it faces the Newburyport Paramounts at the Rye rink. Manager Johnny Carter has announced the starting time as 7:30 o'clock. Weather conditions permitting the Rye club has several interesting games lined up for the weekend.

* * *

THE DOVER Legion will invade the Rye rink next Tuesday night for a playoff of the tie.

Dave Poies of Rye was responsible for sending the game into overtime last night. He rapped the clincher into the Dover nets at 18 minutes in the third period. Frank Ciolek and Phil Drake got assists on the shot which deadlocked the game at 4-4.

In the overtime session Drake sent Rye out in front at the four minute mark when he rapped a shot home. Ciolek got an assist on the play.

Ray McDonough kept the Legionnaires in the game when he tied the count just two minutes before the final bell. The teams decided to forego the sudden death playoff and agreed to meet next Tuesday night for the decision.

* * *

DICK WILSON opened the scoring parade with an unassisted goal after six minutes of play in the opening period. However, Columbo tied the count at the 15 minute mark. Dover went ahead in the second period but Wilson scored his second goal of the night with assists going to Carter and Peyser for the tieing goal.

Dover again went out in front in the third period as Dinny Fogarty rapped a goal past Chuck Sullivan. Wilson tied the game and Johnny Gitschier put the Legionnaires out again as he scored in 15 minutes. Three minutes later Boies got his goal which sent the game into the extra session.

The summary:

RYE	DOVER LEGION
Sullivan, g	g, Callahan
Colliton, rd	rd, McDonough
Belmont, ld	ld, E. Gitschier
Peyser, rw	rw, D. Fogarty
Carter, c	c, J. Gitschier
Wilson, lw	lw, D. Bolduc

Dover spares: Fortin, Schumaker, O'Kane and Columbo. Rye spares: Boies, Ciolek, Drake, I. Jenness, Kelsey, Hayes, H. Carter, Gene Merrill.

Scoring summary:

FIRST PERIOD

1. Rye—Wilson (Unassisted), 6:00.
2. Dover—Columbo (Unassisted), 15:00.

SECOND PERIOD

3. Dover—Schumaker (Fortin), 8:00.
4. Rye—Wilson (Carter, Peyser), 15:00.

THIRD PERIOD

5. Dover—D. Fogarty (Unassisted), 5:00.
6. Rye — Wilson (Unassisted), 12:00.
7. Dover—J. Gitschier (Unassisted), 15:00.
8. Rye—Boies (Ciolek, Drake), 18:00.

OVERTIME

9. Rye—Drake (Ciolek), 4:00.
10. Dover—McDonough (Unassisted), 8:00.

Penalties: Fogarty, Wilson, Ciolek.

February 4, 1949

Peyser, Ciolek, Drake Pace Rye to 9-3 Victory

Back on home ice for the first time since Dec. 26, the Rye hockey club whipped the Newburyport Paramounts, 9-3, before an enthusiastic crowd of fans at the Rye Beach rink last night.

The game served as a warmup for the Rye club which will tangle with two strong opponents tomorrow and Sunday. Laconia, one of the top teams in the southeastern section of the state, will be in tomorrow night while South Peabody, Mass., sextet will play at 2:30 Sunday afternoon. The Laconia game has been scheduled for 8 o'clock tomorrow.

Dick Peyser, Frank Ciolek and Phil Drake scored two goals apiece last night and the rest of the scoring was divided amongst the other two lines.

* * *

NEWBURYPORT was the first to rip the cords as LeBlanc swished one past Chuck Sullivan in 3:29. Rye had been the aggressor before this shot and the Beach sextet stormed down the ice for three goals in the remaining minutes of the first period.

Rye scored twice in the second while the Paramounts tallied once. Going into the final period, Rye was leading, 5-2, and it scored four straight times before the Bay Staters could smack one past Sullivan.

Both goalies played fine defensive games. Sullivan had 22 saves while Bradbury had 15 and nine Rye shots slipped past him.

The summary:

RYE	NEWBURYPORT
Sullivan, g	g, Bradbury
Colliton, rd	rd, N. Marsolais
Jenness, ld	ld, Nichols
Peyser, rw	rw, LeBlanc
J. Carter, c	c, Notarglacomo
Wilson, lw	lw, Poulin

Newburyport spares: R. Marsolais, B. Marsolais, Dumont, Ogden, Columbo, Jancewicz. Rye spares: Belmont, I. Jenness, Boles, Ciolek, H. Carter, Hayes, Redden, Drake, Kelsey, Merrill.

FIRST PERIOD

1. Newburyport—LeBlanc (Unassisted), 3:29.
2. Rye—Boles (Unassisted), 7:46.
3. Rye—Peyser (Wilson, J. Carter), 13:03.
4. Rye—H. Carter (Kelsey), 16:37.

SECOND PERIOD

5. Newburyport—Notarglacomo (Poulin, Dumont), 2:40.
6. Rye—Ciolek (Unassisted), 7:57.
7. Rye—Wilson (J. Carter), 19:43.

THIRD PERIOD

8. Rye—Ciolek (Boles), 8:21.
9. Rye—Drake (Wilson), 9:38.
10. Rye—Peyser (Unassisted), 9:57.
11. Rye—Drake (Unassisted), 14:31.
12. Newburyport—Jancewicz (Unassisted), 19:01.

Penalties: LeBlanc, Hayes, Drake.

February 7, 1949

Rye Hockey Club Ties Strong Bay State Team

HOCKEY THIS WEEK

Tomorrow—Dover Legion at Rye

Wednesday—Rye at St. Jean's Manchester

Thursday — Westbrook Crusaders at Rye

Friday—St. Andre's of Biddeford at Rye

Saturday—Dover Mohawks at Rye

Sunday—Wolfeboro at Rye

Dropping a 2-1 thriller to the Laconia hockey club Saturday night, the Rye Hockey club yesterday afternoon came from behind to tie the South Peabody, Mass., sextet, 4-4, in a fast game played at the Rye Beach rink.

The Rye boys face a busy week as they are scheduled to play every night until Sunday when they meet Wolfeboro in the afternoon.

The several hundred fans who were on hand for the Saturday game saw one of the best contests ever played on Rye ice. The Laconia goalie, Bud Richardson, saved the day for his team as Rye forwards continually pressed to the attack.

* * *

LACONIA scored first when F. Lamire ripped the cords in 8:00 of the second period. Thirty seconds later Dick Peyser sank the equalizer with Dick Wilson and Johnny Carter getting assists.

Laconia, the senior Class B champions of New Hampshire, scored the final goal in 16.00 of the final period as Enwright caught the Rye defensemen too far forward and flipped the puck past Chuck Sullivan.

While Saturday's game was very tight, yesterday was just the opposite. Peabody caught Rye three times in the opening quarter as Kupranic, Perlan and Evitts tallied unassisted goals. Johnny Carter scored for Rye in 14:03.

Peabody took a 4-1 lead in the eleventh minute of the second period as Traccia scored. However, Leighton Remick took a pass from Dave Boles to dump the second Rye counter into the Bay Stater's net.

Frank Ciolek scored the third goal for Rye after an assist from Boles and Dick Wilson knotted the count at 9:20. Johnny Carter assisted him on that play. South Peabody declined to play an overtime period.

The Portsmouth Herald, Portsmouth, N. H.
Monday Evening, February 14, 1949

Boies Scores Three For Rye Pucksters In Rout of Dover

HOCKEY THIS WEEK

Tomorrow—Gloucester at Rye
Wednesday—Dover Arrows at Rye
Thursday—Wolfeboro at Rye
Friday—Rye at Dover Mohawks
Saturday—Rye at Laconia
Sunday—Danvers at Rye (night)

Turning the hat trick is becoming a common feature of Rye hockey games this season.

Dave Boies, who scored thrice in a single game earlier in the week performed the same stunt Saturday night as the Rye Beach club defeated the Dover Mohawks, 9-5, on the beach rink.

Dave, however, had to take a back seat as Buddy McCann of Dover counted four times by sliding the puck past Bob Sullivan, Rye goalie.

Rye scored five times in the opening period after Dover had opened the session by dropping a goal in 2:25. The Mohawks scored first in the second period, too, as McCann slid one past Sullivan in 25 seconds.

The summary:

RYE	DOVER MOHAWKS
Sullivan, g	g, Simpson
W. Jenness, rd	rd, Burns
I. Jenness, ld	ld, Randall
J. Carter, c	c, Clark
Peyser, lw	lw, Martin
Wilson, rw	rw, McCann

Rye spares: Boies, Ciolek, Drake, Belmont, Colliton, Hayes, Kelsey, Hoyt, Remick and H. Carter. Dover spares: Davis, DiMambro, Couser, Meserve.

FIRST PERIOD

1. Dover—Davis (Couser), 2:25.
2. Rye—Boies, 3:20.
3. Rye—Wilson, 7:03.
4. Rye—Wilson (J. Carter), 7:38.
5. Rye—Boies. 8:15.
6. Rye—Colliton, 12:54.
Penalties—Burns, board check.

SECOND PERIOD

7. Dover—McCann (Martin), 0:25.
8. Dover—McCann (Clark), 2:20.
10. Rye—Ciolek. 11:30.
Penalties—Meserve, tripping.

THIRD PERIOD

11. Dover—McCann, 2:40.
12. Dover—McCann, 3.55.
13. Rye—Hoyt (Kelsey, Hayes), 4:52.
14. Rye—Boies, 12:45.
Penalties—Clark, board check.
Officials: Sweetser and Lorenz.

The Portsmouth Herald, Portsmouth, N. H.
Tuesday Evening, September 20, 1949

Sport City

By BOB KENNEDY

ANOTHER Portsmouth young man has come into the working world as a three-sport coach.

Up in little Enfield high, on the fringes of Hanover, Tommy Ahearn of Daniels street has launched a teaching and coaching career.

One of Portsmouth high's football greats of 10 years ago, Tommy played football at Dartmouth during the war and later at UNH. However, he found it necessary to devote most of his time to studies so he gave up the sport he loved.

Tom was graduated from the university last June and made his connections at the small upstate high school during the summer months. He probably will have half a dozen football games, 20 basketball games and 15 baseball games to worry about.

The setup at Enfield should be a good one for the young UNH grad who is seeking experience in the teaching and coaching field. Enfield had a mighty fine baseball team last season and it lost to Towle of Newport in a playoff for one of the berths in the state tournament.

It's track team was good, too. The young Enfield runners came to the Clipper Relays at Portsmouth and made a good showing. Tommy, however, will not have to worry about track but it shows that the calibre of athletes in the small school will make his work pleasant.

* * *

CONDITION exercises for the Rye Hockey club may get underway sooner than they have before.

Business Manager Johnny Carter keeps looking out the bank windows seeking signs of freezing weather.

Someone mentioned a Canadian front to him last summer and he has been looking for a guest from Canada ever since.

The Rye club may have a few changes this year. The playing positions heretofore kept open solely for Rye residents and original founders of the club, may be opened to permit enough additional players to strengthen the club for its major games against such clubs as the Sacred Heart of Concord, Berlin and so forth.

Everyone will continue to have the same chance to play hockey but the additional strength will mean that the club will have greater chances of coming in on the long end of the hockey scores.

The group plans few changes in the rink this year. It will remain beside the road at Rye Beach for this winter, anyway. Another year the players hope to move inland a little to get away from the salt fog and spray which results from the high tides.

* * *

January 9, 1950

Rye Hockey Club Opens Home Schedule Tonight

Rye Hockey club opened its 1950 schedule last night with a 6-4 victory over Gloucester and tonight moves to its home rink to tangle with the strong Newburyport sextet at 8 o'clock.

Dick Wilson scored four goals for the Rye team while Johnny Carter and Phil Drake each scored one in the game played at the new Lynn sports arena.

The frigid weather over the weekend did the job for the Rye hockey players. The ice in the rink at Rye Beach was given four coverings of water over the weekend and each one froze beautifully.

This morning the surface was like glass, according to observers.

The week's schedule, announced this morning by Carter, has Dover coming here Wednesday night and Gloucester Thursday. Friday night the Rye boys go to Westbrook and Saturday the locals go to Laconia. Lynnfield comes to Rye next Sunday afternoon.

Tentative starting lineup for the game tonight will have Meyer in the Rye net, Colliton and W. Jenness at defensive positions while Ciolek, Carter and Wilson will be in the starting line. These positions, however, are very tentative as some of the players may have to miss this first engagement at the Rye rink. The spares are Bill Lorenz, Irving Jenness, Harlan Carter, Phil Drake, Guy Kelsey, Poinier, Hoyt, Peyser, Joe Belmont and Bob Lovett.

PORTSMOUTH, N. H., THURSDAY EVENING, JANUARY 12, 1950

Eight Goals in Last Period Give Rye Second Victory

Capturing its second decision in as many nights, Rye Hockey club came from behind to whip the Newburyport Paramount Jewelers, 9-4, at the Rye rink last night.

Trailing 4-1 at the end of the second period, Rye scored eight times in the last canto to ice the verdict.

Newburyport scored all its goals in the first period as the Rye defenses were not quite up to par. However, the winners rallied and staged one of their best comebacks in their short history.

The second period was scoreless but Rye began pouring the puck into the net at 9:20 of the third frame. Dick Wilson broke the scoring drought with a nice shot after taking a pass from Johnny Carter.

He brought Rye to within one of equalizing when he drove in unassisted in 10:36. Phil Drake scored the tying goal in 13 minutes and Poinier put Rye ahead after a pass from Drake in 14:40.

Newburyport never was in the game after that as Lorenz, Carter, Ciolek and Poinier all scored more goals for the winners.

Rye was not penalized although Newburyport received six, including one for misconduct.

The summary:

RYE	G	NEWBURYPORT
Meyer	RD	Duffy
Colliton	LD	Nichols
H. Carter	C	LeBlanc
J. Carter	LW	Poullin
Ciolek	RW	Giguere
Wilson		McBurnie

Rye spares: W. Jenness, Hoyt, Peyser, Lovett, I. Jenness, Poinier, Kelsey, Drake, Lorenz, Boles. Newburyport spares: Plouff, Gamelin, Jones, Sarty, Ogden, Jancewicz, Pond, Chatigny.

First period: Gamelin (N), 11:39; Jancewicz (N), 12:51; Wilson (R) from Carter, 14:08, Gamelin (N), 13:20; Sarty (N), 18:04.

Rye Swamps Cyclones, Plays Lynn GE Tonight

*RYE		LYNN GE
Meyer	G	Sonier
Colliton	RD	Gunning
W. Jenness	LD	Foster
J. Carter	C	W. Dougherty
Ciolek	LW	Livingston
R. Wilson	RW	J. Dougherty

Game at 8 o'clock

Fresh from its second victory over a strong Biddeford team, the Rye Hockey club will tangle with the Lynn General Electric Co. sextet on the Rye ice tonight.

The Rye boys drubbed the Biddeford Cyclones, rated as the No. 1 team in the Maine city, 11-1, before a thoroughly chilled crowd at Rye Beach last night.

Rye skated to an 11-0 lead before Biddeford managed to poke one into the winner's nets. Dick Wilson scored three goals for the Rye team as did Jack Lorenz.

The night before Rye set back the Biddeford Silver Skates, 6-5, at Biddeford and last night's victory was nectar for the Beach club which has long been a victim of Biddeford teams.

The summary:

RYE		BIDDEFORD
Meyer	G	Frechette
Colliton	RD	Dauphin
W. Jenness	LD	Poissant
J. Carter	C	Boucher
Ciolek	LW	Dubuc
R. Wilson	RW	Gobeil

Rye spares: Drake, Poinier, Peyser, Jenness, Lorenz, Hoyt, Belmont, H. Carter, Lovett, Kelsey. Biddeford spares: Gagne, Sheltra, Champoux, Frechette, P. Camire, Grenier, Neault, Roberge and Mann.

Penalties: Belmont 2, H. Carter, Frechette, Dubuc, Mann.

The score by periods:

	1	2	3	Tot.
Rye	4	5	2	11
Biddeford	0	0	1	1

The scoring:

FIRST PERIOD

1. Rye—Wilson (Ciolek), 1:12.
2. Rye—Colliton, 2:06.
3. Rye—Lorenz, 2:30.
4. Rye—Peyser (Drake), 15:13

SECOND PERIOD

5. Rye—Lorenz (Drake), 6:27.
6. Rye—Ciolek (Carter), 15:38.
7. Rye—Wilson (Carter), 16:13.
8. Rye—Drake (Lorenz), 18:25.
9. Rye—Poinier (Lorenz), 18:52.

THIRD PERIOD

10. Rye—Wilson, 4:11.
11. Rye—Lorenz (Drake), 8:55.
12. Biddeford—Grenier, 10:25.

Officials: Sweetser and Trueman. Scorer: Chub Wilson.

The Portsmouth Herald, Portsmouth, N. H.
Monday Evening, January 23, 1950

Rye Hockey Team Splits With Bay State Sextets

Rye Hockey club outskated the Lynnfield Knights to gain a 4-2 decision yesterday afternoon as well as even a weekend series with teams from the Bay State city. Saturday night the Lynn General Electric team made up a 4-1 deficit and edged the Rye team, 5-4, at the Rye Beach rink.

Defensive play of Goalie Pete Meyer of Rye was outstanding as was the play of Bill Jenness both on defense and offense.

The weekend series brought Rye's total of three victories in their last four starts with their next game coming Wednesday against St. Anselm's in Manchester. The Beach sextet defeated the college team in Harvest hockey league play at the Lynn Arena last fall.

* * *

RYE JUMPED to a 3-0 advantage in the Saturday night game against the GE team. Johnny Carter took a pass from Frank Ciolek to bounce a shot past Sonier in 39 seconds of the first period. Poinier and Guy Kelsey also scored before Lynn could make its first goal, a shot by G. Gunning in 10:46 of the second period.

The losers apparently iced the game in that second period as Phil Drake scored the fourth goal in 15:46 taking an assist from Poinier.

The GE team then began to shoot as the Gunning brothers accounted for three of the four scores either in assists or actual tallying of the points.

Yesterday afternoon the Rye boys spotted Lynnfield a goal in the first period. Johnny Carter sank the equalizer in 3:43 of the second period and broke the tie less than a minute later. Rye then went on to win easily.

The Rye summaries:

SATURDAY GAME

RYE		LYNN GE
Meyer	G	Sonier
W. Jenness	LD	G. Gunning
Colliton	RD	V. Gunning
J. Carter	C	J. Fox
Ciolek	LW	Livingstone
Wilson	RW	J. Doherty

Rye spares: Hoyt, Drake, Peyser, Poinier, Kelsey, Lorenz, I. Jenness and H. Carter. Lynn spares: Phaneuf, C. Muse, Fotte, Celona, Thyberg, Robinson, Warry, Fisher and Lundgren.

The score by periods:

	1	2	3	Tot.
Lynn GE	0	1	4	5
Rye HC	2	2	0	4

The scoring:

FIRST PERIOD
1. Rye—J. Carter (Ciolek), 0:39.
2. Rye—Poinier (Lorenz), 19:30.

SECOND PERIOD
3. Rye—Kelsey (I. Jenness), 2:08.
4. Lynn—Gunning, 10:46.
5. Rye—Drake (Poinier), 15:40.

THIRD PERIOD
6. Lynn—Lundgren, 0:47.
7. Lynn—V. Gunning (G. Gunning), 1:30.
8. Lynn—V. Gunning, 7:56.
9. Lynn—G. Gunning, 12:55.

Penalties: Warry (tripping) and Belmont (tripping).
Officials: Ray Trueman, referee. P. Jenness, scorer. P. Oeser, timer.

SUNDAY GAME

RYE		LYNNFIELD
Meyer	G	Weeks
W. Jenness	RD	H. Rayburn
Colliton	LD	B. Hammer
J. Carter	C	D. Weeks
Ciolek	LW	B. Rayburn
Wilson	RW	B. Weeks

Rye spares: Poinier, Drake, Peyser, Hoyt, I. Jenness, Kelsey and H. Carter. Lynn: E. Melanson, B. Rayburn, L. Clay, B. Howard, Taylor and Morton.

The score by periods:

	1	2	3	Tot.
Rye	0	3	1	4
Lynnfield	1	1	0	2

The scoring:

FIRST PERIOD
1. Lynnfield—D. Weeks, 0:52.

SECOND PERIOD
2. Rye—J. Carter (I. Jenness), 3:34.
3. Rye—J. Carter (Wilson and Ciolek), 4:35.
4. Rye—W. Jenness (J. Carter), 12:57.
5. Lynnfield—R. Weeks, 16:30.

THIRD PERIOD
6. Rye—Ciolek, 11:51.
Penalties: Morton 2, Drake 2, R. Weeks, I. Jenness, H. Weeks, Lorenz, H. Carter.
Officials: Ray Trueman, referee. Chub Wilson, scorer.

PORTSMOUTH, N. H., FRIDAY EVENING, JANUARY 27, 1950

HOTTEST MID-WINTER DAY ON RECORD—Coat off and coat open, Evelyn Elsden and Louise Campbell walk under useless snow-loading equipment yesterday, stored on a downtown street in Boston, as the temperature hit a record 72 degrees. This was highest mark ever recorded for any of the winter months of December, January and February. The snow loaders haven't been used yet this season.

PORTSMOUTH, N. H., SATURDAY EVENING, FEBRUARY 4, 1950

Rye Hockey Club Enters Manchester Tournament

Four of New Hampshire's strong amateur hockey teams will meet in Manchester Sunday for competition in the Senior "B" tournament, sponsored by the St. Jean Maple Leafs of the Queen City.

Rye hockey club is one of the four teams in the play this season. The Beachsters have one of the strongest "B" clubs in the state and should give a good account of themselves at the Manchester tournament.

Weather conditions are the only problems facing the sponsors of the tournament. Rain or sleet would ruin the skating, which is reported to be fairly good right now. St. Jean's rink is open but stands for spectators are covered.

The competition includes the Maple Leafs as well as the Dover Legion and the Laconia Hockey club and Rye.

Semi-finals are scheduled for Sunday afternoon at 2 o'clock, finals in the evening at 8.

Winner of the local tournament will compete in the New England championship at the Boston Garden sometime in March, it was announced by Perry A. Foster of Manchester, tourney director. Starting lineups and pairings for the tourney will be announced tomorrow, Foster stated.

Officials who will handle the Manchester games are Referee Russ Martin of Boston; Linesmen Norm Dufour of Manchester and Hank McLaughlin of Belmont; Timekeeper Billy Marran of Manchester and Announcer Emile Charron, also of Manchester.

February 4, 1950

Rye Hockey Team Drubs Biddeford Flyers, 10-1

Spotting their opponents the first goal of the game, the Rye Hockey club defeated the Silver Skate Flyers of Biddeford, 10-1, at the Maine team's rink last night.

Poinier and Wilson scored three goals apiece for the Rye club while Frank Ciolek hit twice and Harlan Carter and "Peanut" Colliton one apiece.

The lop-sided score makes the game more or less of an upset. Rye-Biddeford clashes of past seasons have been unusually close but this season the Beach sextet has been outscoring the Biddeford teams by half a dozen goals.

Gagne of Biddeford scored first when he drove in to tally unassisted in 15:40 of the first period. Just 70 seconds later Rye tied the score when Poinier took a pass from Phil Drake to drive the equalizer into the nets. Johnny Carter then passed to Ciolek in 20:20 to give Rye the lead it never relinquished.

The summary:

RYE		SILVER SKATES
Kelsey	G	LaJeunesse
Colliton	LD	Nadeau
W. Jenness	RD	Lottinville
Ciolek	LW	LaChance
J. Carter	C	R. Goulet
Wilson	RW	Hodge

Rye spares: Drake, Poinier, Lorenz, I. Jenness, H. Carter, Hoyt, Peyser.
Silver Skates: Hevey, Fournier, Morin, Gregoire, Payeur, Gagne and Guay.

The scoring:

FIRST PERIOD

1-Flyer—Gagne, 15:40
2-Rye—Poinier (Drake), 16:50
3-Rye—Ciolek (J. Carter), 20:20

No penalties

SECOND PERIOD

4-Rye—Poinier, (Lorenz, Peyser), 1:00
5-Rye—Wilson, 6:00
6-Rye—Ciolek, 19:15
7-Rye—Wilson, (penalty-shot), 20:00
8-Rye—Poinier, 23:33

Penalties

R. Goulet—Tripping
R. Goulet—Boardcheck
Payeur—Tripping

Saves

Flyer—9   Rye—7

THIRD PERIOD

9—H. Carter (Ciolek), 5:05
10—Wilson (J. Carter), 21:21
11—Colliton (Wilson), 22:50

Penalties

Nadeau—Tripping
Hoyt—Elbow check
R. Goulet—Tripping

Saves

Flyers—13   Rye—7

Total-Saves

Flyers—35   Rye—24

The Portsmouth Herald, Portsmouth, N. H.,
Monday Evening, February 6, 1950

Rye Edges Wolfeboro, 8-7, In Town Carnival Feature

Coming from behind in the final period, Rye Hockey club defeated the Wolfeboro Indians, 8-7, in the feature contest of the annual Wolfeboro winter carnival yesterday afternoon.

Playing on a smooth, hard surface, Rye's passing attack worked well during the game and paid off in the late minutes when the pressure was on the home club.

The teams swapped goal for goal in the first period with Dick Wilson being the first man to shoot the puck into the nets. His goal came in 6:02 after an assist from Johnny Carter. Clough tied it for Wolfeboro but Bill Lorenz put the Rye boys out in front again in 8:20. Rooney tied the game and J. Carter gave Rye the lead again as he took a pass from Wilson in 15:19. Just before the end of the session, Wolfeboro tied the game.

The Indians took a 6-5 lead in the second period when they scored three goals in the late minutes.

Johnny Carter scored the equalizer in 4:29 of the third period with Wilson and Ciolek getting assists. Hale sent Wolfeboro ahead by one goal only to set the stage for the final Rye attack.

Peyser drove into the Wolfeboro goal to score unassisted in 9:20 and Ned Poinier sank the winning goal two and a half minutes later. The Rye defensemen held off the late drives by the losers and only some fine work by the home team's goalie saved the score from mounting.

Meyer had 24 saves while Jutras had 33.

Score by periods:

	1	2	3	Tot
Rye	3	2	3	8
Wolfeboro	3	3	1	7

Officials: Roger Gregory, referee. Jack Lorenz, scorer.

The summary:

RYE		WOLFEBORO
Meyer	G	Jutras
W. Jenness	RD	Dunham
Colliton	LD	Hale
J. Carter	C	Rooney
Ciolek	LW	Clough
Wilson	RW	Foss

Rye spares: Poinier, Peyser, Lorenz, Hoyt, Kelsey, Belmont, H. Carter and I. Jenness. Wolfeboro spares: Lovering, Grant, Stevens, Melanson, Massey.

FIRST PERIOD

1. Rye—Wilson (J. Carter), 6:02.
2. Wolfeboro—Clough (Rooney), 7:12.
3. Rye—Lorenz (Poinier), 8:20.
4. Wolfeboro—Rooney, 10:45.
5. Rye—J. Carter (Wilson), 15:19.
6. Wolfeboro—Stevens (Rooney), 17:38.

SECOND PERIOD

7. Rye—Colliton (Hoyt), 8:04.
8. Rye—J. Carter (Ciolek), 12:41.
9. Wolfeboro — Foss (Clough), 15:01.
10. Wolfeboro—Clough, 17:42.
11. Wolfeboro — Foss (Rooney), 18:14.

THIRD PERIOD

12. Rye—J. Carter (Wilson Ciolek), 4:29.
13. Wolfeboro—Hale (Foss), 8:51.
14. Rye—Peyser, 9:20.
15. Rye—Poinier (Lorenz, Peyser), 11:53.

Penalties: H. Carter, charging; Jones, slashing, and H. Carter, leg check.

Portsmouth Herald, Portsmouth, N. H.
y Evening, February 27, 1950

Rye Hockey Club Wins Two Weekend Struggles

Winning a pair of major victories over the weekend, the Rye hockey club enjoyed the best ice of the year at its home rink yesterday afternoon and at Suncook on Saturday night.

Rye edged Suncook, 3-2, Saturday and the Dover Mohawks, 4-3, yesterday.

Pete Meyer was outstanding in the nets for the winners as he made brilliant saves in both battles.

Rye passed well against the Mohawks and had several sure scores broken up by Meserve who did a fine job in the Dover cage.

Defensively Rye was tops as Bill Jenness and "Peanut" Colliton broke up the Dover rushes which were sparked by Johnny Gitschier and Dinny Fogarty.

Lorenz got credit for scoring the winning goal but Hoyt actually took the puck through the defensive line. Hoyt skated through Randall and Burns and took a shot at Meserve. The puck bounced against the post and back to Lorenz' stick. A shot snapped the puck into the nets for the goal.

Rye was the victim of an unfortunate deflection at Suncook. The puck bounced off Colliton's skate and into the Rye net with Plourde of Suncook getting credit for a goal. That goal put Rye behind, 2-1, but the third period attack with Ciolek and Johnny Carter scoring, saw the Beach pucksters come through.

The games were very fast and play torrid.

RYE		SUNCOOK
Meyer	G	A. C'rt'm'nche
Colliton	RD	Douval
W. Jenness	LD	Emond
J. Carter	C	C. Noel
Ciolek	LW	E. Noel
Wilson	RW	Plourde

Rye spares: Poinier, Drake, Peyser, I. Jenness, H. Carter, Belmont, Hoyt, Kelsey. Suncook: Bouchard, Janelle, Houle, Gagne, Stokes, Desrocher, E. Courtemanche, Allaire and Demers.

Score by periods:

	1	2	3	Tot.
Rye	1	0	2	3
Suncook	1	1	0	2

FIRST PERIOD
1. Suncook—Bouchard (Plourde), 7:15.
2. Rye—Colliton, 15:10.

SECOND PERIOD
3. Suncook—Plourde, 11:40.

THIRD PERIOD
4. Rye—Ciolek (Wilson), 4:27.
5. Rye—Carter (Wilson), 16:00.

Penalties: Drake (Roughing), Janelle (Roughing) and Poinier (Tripping).

Officials: R. Noel and Labbe.

RYE		MOHAWKS
Meyer	G	Meserve
W. Jenness	RD	Randall
J. Colliton	LD	Burns
J. Carter	C	Fogarty
Ciolek	LW	Renstrom
Wilson	RW	Dimambro

Rye spares: Belmont, Hoyt, Kelsey, Poinier, Peyser, Lorenz, I. Jenness, H. Carter and Drake. Dover Mohawks: McNally, McCann, Dickinson, Bolduc, J. Gitschier, E. Gitschier.

Score by periods:

	1	2	3	Tot.
Rye	2	1	1	4
Dover	2	1	0	3

FIRST PERIOD
1. Dover—Fogarty, 1:31.
2. Rye—J. Carter (Ciolek), 12:50.
3. Rye—Ciolek (Wilson), 13:19.
4. Dover—McNally (Bolduc), 15:13.

SECOND PERIOD
5. Rye—Poinier (Drake, Peyser), 12:55.
6. Dover—Dickinson, 18:40.

THIRD PERIOD
7. Rye—Lorenz (Hoyt), 10:46.

Saves: Rye 30, Dover 32.

Penalties: Burns (Charging).

Officials: Jack Sweetser, referee, and Chub Wilson, scorer.

Rye, Laconia Hockey Winners

Rye Hockey club defeated the Dover Legion, 6-0, and Laconia Hockey club trimmed the St. Jean Maple Leafs, 3-1, at the Manchester rink yesterday.

Laconia and Rye will go to Boston to play off for the New Hampshire Class B championship as a preliminary contest to one of the Boston Olympics' games.

It was the brilliant play of Goalie Peter Meyer which gave the Rye team its inspiration. Dick Wilson's turning the hat trick didn't hurt the Rye cause either. Wilson poured all his goals through the net in the third period.

Two of them were unassisted and one came as the result of a pass from Johnny Carter.

It was Carter who opened the scoring for the Rye team with a goal in six minutes of the first period. It was unassisted. Ned Poinier scored the second goal in 14:30 when he took a pass from Dick Peyser and Phil Drake on a combination.

Poinier scored the third goal in the second period when Irving Jenness gave him a pass in five minutes.

The summary:

RYE	DOVER
Wilson, rw	lw, J. Gitschier
Ciolek, lw	rw, Dennis Fogarty
Carter, c	c, D. Fogarty
Jenness, rd	ld, E. Gitscher
Colliton, ld	rd, Schoonmaker
Meyer, g	g, Meserve

Rye spares: Drake, Poirier, Lorenz, I. Jenness, Hoyt, Kelsey, Belmont, Carter, Peyser.

Dover spares: Bolduc, Clark, Foster, McCann, Berry, Burns.

Scoring:

First Period

1—Rye, Carter unassisted, 6:00
2—Rye, Poirier, assists Peyser, Drake), 14:30

Second Period

3—Rye, Poirier, assist I. Jenness), 5:00

Third Period

4—Rye, Wilson, unassisted, 0:24
5—Rye, Wilson (assist Carter), 8:23
6—Rye, Wilson, unassisted, 13:46
Penalties: Wilson, cross check; Fogarty, slashing.

Referee, Russ Martin; linesman, Norm Dufour.

March 1, 1950

Peyser Sinks Three As Rye Sextet Trims Dover, 6-3

With Dick Peyser turning the "Hat Trick", Rye Hockey club defeated the short-handed Dover Legion, 6-3, in a blinding snowstorm at the Rye Beach rink last night.

Ice conditions were perfect for the game but snow on the ice spoiled the passing attack for both teams. However, it aided Dover because the Legionnaires appeared with but eight players. Had the game been fast, the score might have been doubled.

Peyser scored his three goals in the first and second periods. His first two in the opening period came on assists from Phil Drake while the third was a solo in 11 minutes of the second period. Dover came within one of equalizing in that session but Rye pulled away again in the third period.

The summary:

RYE		DOVER LEGION
Meyer	G	Bolduc
H. Carter	RD	McCann
I. Jenness	LD	J. Gitschier
J. Carter	C	Clark
Ciolek	LW	Fogarty
Wilson	RW	O'Kane

Rye spares: Drake, Kelsey, Peyser, W. Jenness, Poinier and Lorenz. Dover spares: Foster and Berry.

Score by periods:

	1	2	3	Tot.
Rye	3	2	1	6
Dover	0	2	1	3

FIRST PERIOD

1, Rye—Ciolek, 1:50.
2. Rye—Peyser (Drake), 5:45.
3. Rye—Peyser (Drake), 10:25.

SECOND PERIOD

4. Dover—Gitschier (Clark), 3:16.
5. Dover—Fogarty, 9:16.
6. Rye—Peyser, 11:00.

THIRD PERIOD

7. Rye—Wilson, 2:23.
8. Rye—Ciolek (Carter, Wilson), 3:09.
9. Dover—O'Kane, 11:30.

Penalties: Gitschier 2, (pushing and charging), and Foster, tripping.

Officials: Ray Trueman, referee; Sweetser and Carroll, linesman; Chub Wilson, scorer, and P. Oeser, timer.

The Portsmouth Herald, Portsmouth, N. H.
Saturday Evening, March 4, 1950

Rye Hockey Team Trips Gloucester Sextet, 6-3

Rye Hockey club won its second game in as many nights and extended its victory streak as it whipped the Gloucester HC, 6-3, under the lights in Bay State city last night.

Dick Wilson turned the "Hat Trick" for the winners again. He scored three goals for the second night in a row.

Rye's second, fifth and sixth goals were products of his efforts coupled with assists from Frank Ciolek and Johnny Carter.

Rye took a 3-0 lead in the first period and held its advantage throughout the contest.

The Beachtown lads are planning to make the trek to Waterville, Me., this weekend with possible stops in Lewiston tonight and tomorrow to watch the New England amateur championship play at the huge Arena.

The summary:

RYE HC		GLOUCESTER
Kelsey	G	C. Garron
H. Carter	LD	Roberts
I. Jenness	RD	Marchant
J. Carter	C	Wonson
Ciolek	LW	Jussilia
Wilson	RW	Orange

Rye spares: Poinier, Sleeth, Lorenz, Hoyt and Colliton. Gloucester spares: Currier, Morris, Abbott, Harnish, Witham DeCos, Bliss, Swinson and Ahonen.

Score by periods:

	1	2	3	Tot.
Rye	3	1	2	6
Gloucester	0	1	2	3

Rye scoring:
1. Poinier (Sleeth).
2. Wilson (Ciolek).
3. Hoyt (Poinier and Sleeth).
4. Ciolek.
5. Wilson (Carter).
6. Wilson.

Gloucester scoring:
1. Bliss, two.
2. Currier.

March 7, 1950

Aggressive Play Gives Rye Sextet Win Over Suncook

Aggressive hockey proved to be the best defense for the Rye Hockey club as it defeated Suncook, 11-6, at the Rye Beach rink last night.

Scoring five times in the first period, Rye kept the Suncook team off balance for the better part of the game.

* * *

INDIVIDUAL star for the visitors was "Lefty" Jannelle, the 17-year-old chucker who hurled Manchester Post 79 to the New Hampshire Junior Legion baseball championship last year. Janelle scored four goals for the losers and kept them in the game until the final whistle.

Second period scoring was even but Rye again had the advantage in the fourth quarter. All three lines played excellent hockey for the winners. Frank Ciolek played some of his best hockey of the winter as he set Dick Wilson up once and Carter twice.

Carter turned the "Hat Trick" with three goals against the Suncook sextet. Poe Belmont made a nice solo dash in which he split the defense and fired one into the upper corner of the nets past Courtemanche.

* * *

J. CARTER OPENED the scoring after one minute of play. Janelle tied the game a minute later and that was the closest Suncook ever came to the fast skating Rye club.

The summary:

RYE HC		SUNCOOK
Kelsey	G	Courtemanche
Colliton	RD	Dorval
Belmont	LD	N. Emond
J. Carter	C	Janelle
Ciolek	LW	Duhaime
Wilson	RW	Houle

Rye spares: Drake, Poinier, Sleeth, I. Jenness, H. Carter, Lorenz, Hoyt. Suncook spares: C. Noel, A. Plourde, R. Courtemanche, Gagne, Stokes and Duval.

Score by periods:

	1	2	3	Tot.
Rye	5	3	3	11
Suncook	1	3	2	6

FIRST PERIOD

1. Rye—J. Carter (Ciolek), 1:00.
2. Suncook—Janelle, 2:00.
3. Rye—Peyser (Poinier, Drake), 8:00.
4. Rye—Poinier, 10:00.
5. Rye—Poinier (Drake), 10:30.
6. Rye—Belmont, 19:00.

SECOND PERIOD

7. Suncook—Janelle, 1:00.
8. Suncook—Janelle, 7:00.
9. Rye—Wilson, 13:00
10. Suncook—Gagne, 14:30.
11. Rye—Sleeth (Lorenz), 24:00.
12. Rye—Hoyt (Sleeth), 24:45.

THIRD PERIOD

13. Rye—J. Carter (Ciolek), 3:30.
14. Suncook—Stokes, 5:00.
15. Rye—Wilson (Ciolek), 7:50.
16. Suncook—Janelle, 9:30.
17. Rye—J. Carter (Wilson), 20:00.

Penalties: R. Courtemanche, holding; Drake, charging and Plourde, slashing.

Officials: Ray Trueman, referee; Jack Sweetser, linesman, and Chub Wilson, scorer.

PORTSMOUTH, N. H., MONDAY EVENING, MARCH 27, 1950

SOUTHEASTERN CHAMPS—Titlists of the Southeastern New Hampshire and Maine area, Rye Hockey club completed its winter season with a 13-6 mark. The members of the team in the above photo are, left to right, front row: Frank Colliton, Dick Wilson, Dick Peyser, Winn Hoyt, Bill Lorenz, Phil Drake, Ned Poinier. Back row: Harlan Carter, Bill Jenness, John Carter, Pete Meyer, goalie; Irving Jenness, Frank Ciolek, Guy Kelsey and Coach Dave Boies. Ronnie Sleeth, former UNH captain, and Joe Belmont were unable to be present when the photo was taken. (Portsmouth Herald photo)

Rye Loses New Hampshire Title

Losing its first period lead, the Rye Hockey club fell before the Laconia Hockey club, 9-4, in the New Hampshire Class B championship game played Saturday afternoon at Boston Garden.

Dick Wilson turned the hat trick for the Rye club as did "Peanut" Lemire of Laconia. Each player scored three goals in the wild contest on the Garden ice. Rye led 3-2 at the end of the first period but Laconia came back to score five times in the second period and lead, 7-3, going into the last period. It scored twice more before Wilson could collect his third goal of the game and Rye's fourth of the afternoon contest.

The summary:

LACONIA		RYE
Richardson, g		g. Meyer
R. Perry, rd		ld. Jenness
J. Perry, ld		rd. Colliton
Lemire c		c. J. Carter
B. Perry, rw		lw. Ciolek
Dube, lw		rw. Wilson

Laconia spares: Enright, Hickey, Levasseur, Bissonette, Brough, Shaw,

Rye spares: Drake, Poinier, Hoyt, Jenness, Kelley, H. Carter, Peyser.

Scoring:

First Period
1. Laconia, Brough (Bissonette) 3:53.
2. Laconia, Levasseur (Brough) 8:54.
3. Rye, Jenness (Peyser) 15:05.
4. Rye, Wilson (Ciolek) 18:00.
5. Rye, Wilson (Ciolek) 19:43.

Second Period
6. Laconia, Lemire (Shaw) 12:04.
7. Laconia, Bissonette (Levasseur) 16:43.
8. Laconia, Lemire 18:49.
9. Laconia, Enright (Hickey) 19:04.
10. Laconia, Bissonette 19:52.

Third Period
11. Laconia, Lemire (Dube) 2:06.
12. Laconia, Noyes (Enright, Hickey) 2:50.
13. Rye, Wilson (Peyser) 11:40.

Penalties: Jenness, two minutes, elbow; H. Carter, two minutes, roughing, both in third period.

With the Laconia battle, Rye completed its winter schedule but it will compete in one or two more tournaments. It played 19 games

outdoors, winning 13 and losing 6. In the Harvest hockey league at Lynn, Rye split eight games with four wins and four losses.

The combined totals are 17-10 with 142 goals scored by Rye and 100 against, not including Saturday's battle.

After getting away to a very slow start because of the mild and uncertain weather in December and January, by Jan. 22 Rye had played eight games, five of these being played in six days. The difficulties that confront a team relying on outdoor uncovered ice are in evidence in this early uncertain time of the season. A quick cold snap must be utilized in order to build or improve the ice surface, and yet it is often followed by several thawing days which usually undo any work already done. This means that a team has to keep working on the rink whenever there is a cold night or day and hope that some games can be played before bad weather again appears.

Rye encountered its best ice at Wolfeboro on two occasions, winning one and losing the other, each game the same score, 8-7. Rye's best home ice was used but not seen, when they played Dover Legion in a hard snowstorm. The last game against Suncook at Rye also had good ice.

The season's individual scoring marks:

	G	A	T
Wilson	40	13	53
J. Carter	25	22	47
Ciolek	15	24	39
Poinier	15	6	21
Lorenz	12	8	20
Drake	7	13	20
Peyser	7	6	13
Hoyt	3	3	6
Sleeth	3	3	6
Colliton	3	2	5
I. Jenness	1	4	5
Fournier	3	1	4
Belmont	3	0	3
Kelsey	3	0	3
W. Jenness	1	2	3
H. Carter	1	0	1

The Portsmouth Herald, Portsmouth, N. H.
Friday Evening, April 7, 1950

Rye Loses, 2-1, in Sixth Overtime

Rye Hockey club lost a heartbreaker to Lynnfield Knights, 2-1, after six overtime periods in the New England Senior "B" tournament at the North Shore sports Arena in Lynn last night.

The teams battled through one regulation five minute overtime, four scoreless "sudden death" periods and the fifth "sudden death" was nearly over when Lynnfield poked the winning goal past Pete Meyer of Rye.

Lynnfield scored first in the opening period. Dick Wilson took a pass from Frank Ciolek to score the tying goal in the second period.

Both goalies were outstanding in the nets. Meyer played a wonderful game for Rye and the Lynnfield netminder was superb as he broke up several Rye solos. The Rye wings made their way through the Lynn defenses on several occasions for clear shots at the goal but "Buck fever" prevailed in the heat of the contest and the shots were smothered by the goal tender.

Tomorrow afternoon Rye will meet the Weymouth Hockey club in the consolation game at 2 o'clock. Weymouth was beaten by Winchester, 4-2, in the first game last night and Winchester will meet Lynnfield in the championship clash tomorrow.

Rye holds two decisions over the Knights in games played this year but it couldn't quite make it three in a row. Rye edged the Lynnfield team, 3-2, in the Harvest hockey league last fall and 4-2 Jan. 22 on Rye ice.

The Portsmouth Herald, Portsmouth, N. H.
Friday Evening, October 27, 1950

Rye Sextet in League

Gaining an even split in its two starts, Rye Hockey club has again joined the Harvest Hockey league at the Lynn sports arena.

Rye lost its opening game, 6-2, to the Beverly Flyers. Dick Wilson and Frankie Ciolek scored the Rye goals. Play was ragged as neither team had been on the ice since the tournament early last spring.

Last night, however, the Rye team went wild. It defeated the Beverly Farms sextet, 10-1, in one of the highest scoring contests the league has seen. The forward line of the Rye club was red hot. Johnny Carter scored five goals to lead the attack for the New Hampshire skaters.

Also scoring last night was Ciolek, Wilson, Dinny Fogarty, Win Hoyt and Bill Lorenz. The Rye defenses were the best they have been in a couple of seasons and the team showed plenty of power.

Next Tuesday night the Rye club meets the Lynnfield Knights. It was with Lynnfield last spring that Rye played the marathon game. Rivalry between the two clubs is most keen and a large crowd is expected to attend the 9 pm contest.

1951

Nash

AIRFLYTE

The World's Most Modern Cars

COLEMAN NASH CO., Inc.
Tel. 3165
228 Islington St. Portsmouth

January 12, 1951

Rye Seahawks Trounce Suncook, 7-3, in Opener

Rye Hockey club's Seahawks opened their 1951 season by trimming the Suncook sextet, 7-3, on the fast ice of the mid-state town last night. Dick Wilson scored four goals for the Rye club as he outhatted the hatters.

Rye took a 3-0 lead in the first 18 minutes of the game. Suncook then scored twice before Rye managed to come back in the second period and tally twice more to hold a 5-2 lead at the end of the second period.

Rye again outscored its rivals in the third quarter to win handily.

The victory set the stage for the home opener Sunday afternoon with Amesbury. The Bay Staters will come to the new rink in North Hampton for the 2 o'clock clash.

Next Wednesday night the Rye team will travel to Gloucester and a week from Sunday the Suncook team will come to Rye for its return clash with the Seahawks.

In the nets last night, Guy Kelsey played a fine game. It was the first time this winter the defenseman had been shifted into the goal and he kicked a lot of shots aside.

The summary:

Suncook		Rye
French	g	Kelsey
H. Noel	ld	I. Jenness
Duval	rd	H. Carter
C. Noel	c	J. Carter
Demers	lw	Ciolek
F. Noel	rw	Wilson

Rye spares: Lorenz, Drake, Hoyt, Remick. Suncook spares: Kelley, Janelle, Lemire and Christy.

The scoring:

FIRST PERIOD
1. Rye—Carter, 2:15.
2. Rye—Wilson, 11:00.
3. Rye—Ciolek, 15:00.
4. Suncook—Demers, 18:00.

SECOND PERIOD
5. Suncook—H. Noel, 5:48.
6. Rye—Drake, 6:30.
7. Rye—Wilson, 17:40.

THIRD PERIOD
8. Rye—Wilson, 3:00.
9. Rye—Wilson, 10:02.
10. Suncook—Kelley, 16:09.

The Portsmouth Herald, Portsmouth, N. H.
Thursday Evening, January 18, 1951

Rye Seahawks Are Tied by Gloucester Sextet, 5-5

J. Carter Scores Thrice for Town On Foreign Rink

SCHEDULED GAMES
Tomorrow: Suncook at Rye
Sunday: Rye at Laconia
Tuesday: Rye at Biddeford
Wednesday: Amesbury at Rye

Watching a hard-earned rally go by the boards in the closing seconds of a fast contest, the Rye Seahawks played the Gloucester Fishermen to a 5-5 draw on Bay State ice last night.

Rye made up a 4-2 deficit and took a 5-4 lead only to have the Gloucester team tie the contest. The home sextet got away to a 3-0 lead in the first period, although Rye had more than a dozen close shots at Goalie Garron of the Gloucester team.

* * *

ROUGH SNOW and ice on the rink made the job easier for the defensemen because the forwards could not carry the puck without having it bounce all over the ice. Long slap shots were made rather than carry the puck into the goal.

Pearson, playing his first game for Rye, scored the first goal on an unassisted rush. Standing on the offensive blue line, he took the puck and sped through the defensive players in one of the prettiest moves seen at Gloucester ice. He faked the goalie to one side and flipped the puck into the corner.

* * *

THE SECOND RYE goal was a nice effort and combination. Frankie Ciolek, who picked up four assists, started to play the Gloucester zone and he tipped a pass to "Flash" Jenness. Jenness whipped a pass across the goal mouth to Johnny Carter who was uncovered. Carter shot the rubber home.

The Rye defense pairs were Bill Lorenz and Bill Jenness, Harlan Carter and Jack Colliton.

RYE		GLOUCESTER
Meyer	G	Lovett
Lorenz	LD	Tysver
W. Jenness	RD	Garron
J. Carter	C	Bliss
Ciolek	LW	Jusilla
I. Jenness	RW	Witham

Rye spares: Drake, Hoyt, Remick, Kelsey, H. Carter, Colliton, Pearson.

Gloucester spares: Garron, DeCoste, Marchant, Swinson, Abbott, Ahonen, Morris, Harnish and Worthy.

Scoring:

Rye—
1. Pearson (Unassisted)
2. J. Carter (Jenness, Ciolek)
3. Pearson (Ciolek)
4. Carter (Ciolek)
5. Carter (Ciolek)

Gloucester—
1. R. Garron
2. Bliss (Currier)
3. Bliss (R. Garron)
4. Currier (Bliss)
5. Currier (Bliss)

January 24, 1951

Seahawks Trim Biddeford, 7-1

COMING GAMES

Tonight: Game canceled.
Friday—Wolfeboro at Rye
Sunday—Gloucester at Rye

Perfect ice conditions at Biddeford last night saw the Rye Hockey club Seahawks defeat the Silver Skates, 7-1. It was an excellent night for hockey but the rapidly-warming air called a halt to activities today as rain beat down on all rinks.

The forecast of freezing weather in the next few days may give the Rye pucksters a chance to get in weekend games with Wolfeboro and Gloucester.

It was the excellent work of the Silver Skates goalie that kept the score down.

The Rye scoring got underway at the two-minute mark when Dick Wilson scored on a pass from Frank Ciolek. A couple of minutes later, Jack Colliton took the puck from behind his own goal, swept the length of the ice and scored on a shot from 20 feet out.

Two quick goals in the middle of the second period by Flash Jenness, his first of the season, brought the count to 5-0. The first one fished off a rush by Phil Drake and the second was the result of a Lorenz rebound.

Ciolek fired the second goal of his "hat trick" on a pass from Harlan Carter, who sparked the Rye defense. Ciolek added his third tally on a play that started in the Biddeford corner of the rink, Johnny Carter started the play in a pass out to Wilson. Wilson passed to Ciolek who scored easily.

Goalie Pete Meyer of Rye had a shutout all the way.

Rye was two men short late in the third quarter when the Biddeford skaters finally made their way through the defenses to press Meyer. That was their only score of the match.

The third period took 45 minutes to play because of many penalties handed out by the official who had gained his experience under rules other than those pertaining to the amateur circuit. The amateurs play under the NHL rules.

The summary:

Rye Seahawks		Silver Skates
Meyer	G	LaJeunesse
H. Carter	LD	Armstron
W. Jenness	RD	Nadeau
J. Carter	C	B. Goulet
Ciolek	LW	Boucher
Wilson	RW	R. Goulet

Rye spares: Lorenz, Drake, Remick, Hoyt, I. Jenness and Colliton.

Silver Skates: Gagne, Heber, Paquette, Vereneau, Huard, U. Gagne, Fournier, Charette and Guay.

FIRST PERIOD

1. Rye—Wilson (Ciolek).
2. Rye—Colliton.
3. Rye—Ciolek (Carter, Wilson).

SECOND PERIOD

4. Rye—I. Jenness (Drake).
5. Rye—I. Jenness (Lorenz).
6. Rye—Ciolek (H. Carter).

THIRD PERIOD

7. Rye—Ciolek (Carter, Wilson).
8. Silver Skates—U. Gagne.

Penalties: Colliton (Interference), J. Carter (Trip), H. Carter (Board check), Nadeau (Trip), Wilson (High stick), H. Carter (Trip), Lorenz (Misconduct), Goulet, (Charging), Armstrong (Trip) and W. Jenness (Trip).

PORTSMOUTH, N. H., SATURDAY EVENING, FEBRUARY 3, 1951

Rye Pucksters Recover To Nip Gloucester, 5-4

Rye Hockey club Seahawks defeated the Gloucester Hockey club, 5-4, in a fast game played at the North Hampton rink of the New Hampshire sextet.

Friday night the Seahawks played the powerful Wolfeboro team to a 7-7 tie in the upstate town. Despite the fact the game was a high-scoring affair, some magnificent goal tending on the part of both goalies kept the scoring to a minimum.

* * *

WOLFEBORO jumped to a 2-0 lead in the first period. Johnny Carter and Dick Wilson knotted the count only to have the Wolfeboro team go ahead. Remick tied the game at three-all.

In the final period, Wolfeboro went ahead, 7-6, only to have Rye come from behind again and tie the count. Dick Wilson poked one into the far corner of the cage to tie the game.

Yesterday, Rye again spotted the opposition a two goal lead. Remick scored first for the Seahawks and Wilson tied the game in the first period. Then Rye pulled ahead, 3-2, for a short time but Gloucester tied the battle just before the end of the first period.

Drake put Rye ahead in the second period when he scored on Jenness rebound. Gloucester scored its fourth goal on a passout. It happened behind the Rye net and was deflected into the goal by Peter Meyer's stick.

Dick Wilson scored the winning goal on a solo.

* * *

GLOUCESTER also got another clean break just before the game ended. However, the goal was not allowed because a player was offside.

Rye players worked all night spraying the rink to build ice over many of the bare spots. Their efforts were rewarded by a fine playing surface.

The summary:

RYE		GLOUCESTER
Meyer	g	E. Garron
W. Jenness	ld	Witham
H. Carter	rd	Jussila
J. Carter	c	R. Garron
Ciolek	lw	Bliss
Wilson	rw	Tysver

Rye spares: Lorenz, Drake, Hoyt, Remick, Colliton, I. Jenness and Kelsey. Gloucester spares: Morriss, Marchant and Harnisch.

Scoring:

FIRST PERIOD

1. Gloucester—Garron, 6:20.
2. Gloucester—Tysver, 6:12.
3. Rye—Remick (Drake, Hoyt), 11:09.
4. Rye—Wilson (Unassisted), 12:17.
5. Rye—Wilson (Ciolek), 19:10.
6. Gloucester—Marchant, 10:20.

SECOND PERIOD

7. (Rye—Drake (Jenness), 19:40.

THIRD PERIOD

8. Gloucester—R. Garron, 6:30.
9. Rye—Wilson, 15:00.

Officials: Ray Trueman, referee.

PORTSMOUTH, N. H., MONDAY EVENING, MARCH 19, 1951

Rye Defeats Laconia, Nashua

GAMES THIS WEEK

Wednesday: Amesbury, Maples at Rye.

Friday: Amesbury Sacred Heart at Amesbury.

Sunday: Wolfeboro at Rye

Rye Hockey club picked up its sixth and seventh victories of the season when it defeated Laconia and Nashua after the proposed Class B tournament was canceled Saturday night.

The Nashua team was unable to have all its players here for the Saturday game so the tournament was postponed.

Rye defeated Laconia, 5-2, Saturday night as the Lake City pucksters made the trip here early in the evening. The Seahawks then proceeded to whale Nashua Royals, 9-5, yesterday afternoon as the ice conditions remained nearly perfect.

Laconia and Rye played nip and tuck for two periods but the winners exploded for three goals in the third stanza! Bill Lorenz scored twice and "Flash" Jenness made one.

Phil Drake, Bill Lorenz and John Carter scored two goals apiece in their victory yesterday.

Woody Noel, former UNH star who resided in Portsmouth, was sparkplug of the Royals as he played the major portion of the 60 minutes of the game.

The Laconia game:

RYE		LACONIA
Meyer	g	Richardson
W. Jenness	l d	R. Perry
H. Carter	r d	J. Perry
J. Carter	c	Lamere
Ciolek	l w	Poire
Wilson	r w	Dube

Rye spares: Remick, Kelsey, Drake, Colliton, I. Jenness, Lorenz.

Laconia spares: Brough, Hickey, R. Levasseur, N. Levasseur, Fredette and Shaw.

The scoring:

FIRST PERIOD

1. Laconia—Levasseur, 9:00.
2. Rye—Wilson, 11:20.

SECOND PERIOD

3. Laconia—Poire, 13:40.
4. Rye—J. Carter (Wilson), 14:10.

THIRD PERIOD

5. Rye—Lorenz (Drake, I. Jenness), 5:19.
6. Rye—I. Jenness (Drake, Lorenz), 6:05.
7. Rye—Lorenz, 13:45.

Penalties: Brough, cross check; I. Jenness, interference; Hickey, hooking.

The Nashua game:

RYE		NASHUA
Meyer	G	McLoud
W. Jenness	RD	Noel
H. Carter	LD	Gamache
J. Carter	C	Ravenelle
Ciolek	LW	Dionne
Wilson	RW	Callahan

Rye spares: Drake, Remick, Lorenz, Colliton, I. Jenness, Kelsey, Hoyt.

Nashua spares: R. Joyal P. Joyal, Ray Joyal, Zettenberg, Lepine, Brune.

The scoring:

FIRST PERIOD

1. Rye—Wilson, 0:30.
2. Rye—Ciolek (Wilson), 5:19.
3. Rye—Remick (Lorenz), 9:32.
4. Nashua—Rene Joyal (Noel), 14:05.
5. Rye—Lorenz (Remick, Drake), 19:40.

SECOND PERIOD

6. Nashua—Noel, 1:41.
7. Rye—Drake (Remick, H. Carter), 3:42.
8. Nashua—Rene Joyal (Zettenberg), 3:56.
9. Rye—J. Carter (Ciolek), 6:12.
10. Rye—Lorenz (Drake, Remick), 19:19.

THIRD PERIOD

11. Nashua—R. Joyal (P. Joyal), 0:45.
12. Rye—Drake, 2:15.

October 6, 1951

Rye Seahawks Plan Play In Harvest Hockey Loop

Sharpening their skates as the opening of the hockey season is but two weeks away, the Rye Seahawks hope to enter the fast competition of the autumn league in the North Shore Arena at Lynn.

Johnny Carter, manager of the Seahawks, said the boys have been getting into shape during the past couple of weeks and are anxious to finish in the playoffs for the North Shore honors.

The fall loop is called the Harvest league and displays some very good amateur hockey. Last season the Rye team won 4, lost 4, and tied 2, to end up in third place.

With more than a few prayers that their work and patience will be rewarded this year, the team is looking forward to a good out-door ice season. The new rink in North Hampton on Atlantic avenue has recently been graded and seeded, and with reasonably cold weather, will provide the best base on which to build ice.

This year the team expects to be strengthened by some new players. Any hockey players in this area who have had experience on school or amateur teams are encouraged to get in touch with John Carter, manager, in West Rye, or David Boies, coach, in North Hampton.

PORTSMOUTH, N. H., THURSDAY EVENING, NOVEMBER 1, 1951

Seahawks Sharpen Skates For Ice Opener Saturday

Skates honed to a razor edge, the Rye Seahawks will open their hockey season this Saturday night at the North Shore sports arena in Lynn. Mass., as a member of the 12-team Harvest Hockey league.

Strongest amateur sextets in the Boston and Greater Boston area have been included in the popular fall loop this season and the teams will play just once and the playoff at the end of the circuit has been eliminated.

Seven new teams have been added to the roster of the league for the 1951 season. Each team will play 11 games and the club in first place at the end of the season. Nov. 24, will be crowned champion.

This is the third season the Harvest loop has been in operation and it has gained in popularity each year.

The Seahawks' schedule and starting times are as follows:

*Oct 20—Sat., 9 pm. Dedham.
Oct 23—Tues., 7 pm. Medford.
*Oct. 27—Sat., 6 pm. Brookline.
Oct 31—Wed., 6:30 pm, Lynn-field.
*Nov. 3—Sat., 4 pm. Beverly.
Nov. 6—Tues., 7 pm. Beverly Farms.
*Nov. 10—Sat., 10 pm, East Boston.
Nov. 13—Tues., 7 pm, Peabody.
*Nov 17—Sat., 4 pm, Weymouth.
Nov. 22—Thurs., 7 pm, Lynn.
*Nov. 24—Sat., 4 pm, Andover.

*Games start at 4 pm.
Tuesdays games start at 7 pm.

December 3, 1951

'Hawks Ask Santa For 'Little Ice' On Hockey Rink

"Dear Santa—

"Send us a little ice. . . "

"That's the message from south of the Portsmouth border.

Embarking on their fifth season of hockey, the Rye Hockey club Seahawks this winter will play in a New Hampshire Class B, league which will embrace the communities of Laconia, Nashua, Wolfeboro, Suncook, Rye and Dover.

The Seahawks recently completed their season of play in the Harvest Hockey league at the North Shore sports arena in Lynn, Mass., and they finished in seventh place. The early November losing streak reflected in the loss of Richard "Dick" Wilson to the United States Air force.

* * *

WILSON, a high-scoring, scrappy wingman, left in the middle of the season for Texas and a job flying twin-engine bombers. The Seahawks won three, lost six and tied two at Lynn. However, several of the losses were by one goal and came in the closing seconds of play.

In the new Granite State league, the first attempt to organize amateur hockey, teams will play each other at least twice during the regular season. The first two games will provide the basis for the playoff considerations. An attempt to eliminate tie games will be made as managers have agreed to play "sudden-death" overtime periods the length of which is not to exceed 10 minutes.

Manager Johnny Carter of the Seahawks said the tentative opening date for the North Hampton rink is Jan. 11 when the Rye pucksters will meet Laconia at 8 o'clock.

* * *

HOWEVER, there may be one or two games before that time as soon as dates with Suncook and Wolfeboro can be agreed upon. Rye will open its outdoor season at Laconia on Dec. 28. On Jan. 4 they play at Nashua.

Outdoor hockey, especially in the coastal regions, is dependent upon the weather and, "rained-out" contests will be rescheduled and dates announced later.

The members of the team already have been working on their rink at North Hampton and hope to have it in shape before Christmas. The freeze-up last week lent hope to the picture; but the mild weather since that time has brought a halt to all freezing proceedings.

PORTSMOUTH, N. H., THURSDAY EVENING, DECEMBER 27, 1951

Seahawks Edge Amesbury In Overtime Ice Clash

AMESBURY — Frankie Ciolek's "sudden death" goal in 4:45 of the extra period gave the Rye Hockey club Seahawks a 7-6 victory over the Amesbury Sacred Heart sextet in the Massachusetts' city last night.

Two excellent saves by Pete Meyer, Rye goalie, as well as the outstanding play of the forward line gave the Seahawks their victory.

* * *

THE RYE BOYS got off to a fast start by keeping the puck in the Amesbury zone most of the time. Amesbury covered well and fine saves by Goalie Stuart kept the visitors from mounting the score.

Rye's best play of the second period was a wing-to-wing. pass from Ciolek to Phil Drake who fired from just inside the blue line to beat Stuart on a high corner shot. The defensive gem of the game came late in the third period when Levesque broke through the Rye defense to skate into the goal

alone. Meyer came up with the save that forced the game into overtime.

* * *

MEYER ALSO saved Rye in the "sudden death" when another breakthrough occurred and Amesbury had a clear shot at the nets. Pete tussed the puck aside and Rye cleared it from the zone to ride safely to the point when Ciolek took the pass from Johnny Carter for the winning goal.

The Seahawks skated off in the first quarter primed for the kill. They had a 5-1 lead at the end of that session thanks to some excellent shooting. Amesbury caught on in the second period and cut the margin by a goal. Rye led, 6-3, at the end of the second.

* * *

AMESBURY held Rye scoreless in the third period and tallied three times itself to tie the count just before the end of the game.

Ice conditions permitting, Rye will play two games this weekend. Laconia will be met at Laconia Saturday night and Nashua travels to Rye Sunday for Class B league games in the New Hampshire circuit.

The summary:

RYE		AMESBURY
Meyer	G	Stuart
H. Carter	rd	Proulx
I. Jenness	ld	Desboisbriand
J. Carter	c	Levesque
Drake	rw	Fournier
Ciolek	lw	Cloutier

Rye spares: Reynolds, Ducharme, Fogarty, Foster, W. Jenness, LeBlanc. Amesbury spares: Joubert, Michaud, Roy, Gosselin, Crishman, Brochu.

FIRST PERIOD

1. Rye—Ducharme (H. Carter)
2. Rye—LeBlanc
3. Amesbury—Joubert
4. Rye—LeBlanc
5. Rye—H. Carter
6. Rye—Drake (Carter)

Penalties: J. Carter, Levesque, I. Jenness, Drake, LeBlanc, Ducharme.

SECOND PERIOD

7. Amesbury—Roy (Joubert)
8. Amesbury—Joubert
9. Rye—Drake (Ciokle)

Penalties: LeBlanc (Match), Ducharme, H. Carter, Proulx, Brochu.

THIRD PERIOD

10. Amesbury—Levesque
11. Amesbury—Crisham (Gosselin)
12. Amesbury—Michaud (Proulx)

Penaltries: None.

OVERTIME

13. Rye—Ciolek (J. Carter), 4:45.

Penalties: None.

Officials: A. Roy, E. Nichols and I. Wall.

PORTSMOUTH, N. H., SATURDAY EVENING, JANUARY 26, 1952

Wingman of Rye Sextet Slated for Air Force Duty

Richard W. "Dick" Wilson, crack wingman of the Rye Hockey club Seahawks reports for active duty with the United States Air force tomorrow.

A B25 pilot during World War II, Wilson is a first lieutenant. The need for twin-engine pilots has increased during the recent emergency.

Lieutenant Wilson took part in 68 missions over enemy-held islands in the Pacific during the last war. His bombing squadron hit many of the Jap-held islands from Australia to Mindoro.

Wilson was engaged in operations with Sky Spray, Inc., shortly after the war; but, for the past year has been working in the deRochemont productions of motion pictures in the Portsmouth area.

He played hockey with the Rye Seahawks for four seasons and is one of the leading scorers with the team. At the present time the team is playing in the Harvest Hockey league at Lynn, Mass.

Wilson leaves tomorrow for North Carolina and he will be assigned to a training squadron at a locale determined by the air force.

AUTHORIZED
PONTIAC

SALES SERVICE

GUARANTEED
USED CARS
Bear Wheel Alinement
**PORTSMOUTH
MOTOR MART**
253 Middle St.   Phone 22

PORTSMOUTH, N. H., WEDNESDAY EVENING, JANUARY 30, 1952

EYES RIGHT—Goalie Pete Meyer of the Rye Hockey club Seahawks is casting a wary eye for the loose puck, which may be traveling his way with great rapidity. The Rye sextet will take to the ice again tomorrow night at 8 o'clock in Nashua. The Seahawks return home, ice permitting, on Sunday afternoon and will meet the Wolfeboro Bears at 5 o'clock on the North Hampton ice. (Portsmouth Herald photo)

Rye, Dover Legion Tie, 3-3

DOVER — Playing their second game in as many nights, the Dover Legion tied the Rye Seahawks, 3-3, on the Cochecotown rink in sub-freezing temperatures.

Rye was leading 2-1 in the second period when the Legionnaires staged the rally which won them the ball game. Dover was fresh from a 4-3 victory over the Nashua Royals and eager to gain a win from Rye.

* * *

THREE UNASSISTED goals marked Rye's effort. The condition of the ice made it difficult to work any smooth plays and passes. It was hard but had been cut up quite badly before the game because of general skating.

Guy Kelsey was given good support in protecting the nets. Kelsey had 18 saves while Phil Meserve had 27 for the Legion. Kelsey saved what might have been the winning goal in the closing minutes of the third period when he caught a shot which had the speed of a bullet.

* * *

HOMER JOHNSON, one of Rye's new players, did a nice job in defense. Johnson is playing his first organized hockey and has learned quickly. He cleared the puck neatly and quickly as well as fighting hard in the corners.

Rye was slightly short handed so the linemen and defensemen had many chances to swap positions and nearly everyone played at least four-fifths of the game.

The summary:

Meserve	g	Kelsey
Crowley	rd	H. Carter
McNally	ld	I. Jenness
Dan Fogarty	c	J. Carter
Bolduc	lw	Ciolek
McCann	rw	Peters

Dover spares: Hockman, Hester, Din Fogarty, Laville, Sears, Dolan. Rye spares: Remick, W. Jenness and Johnson.

The scoring:

FIRST PERIOD
1. Dover—McCann (12:00).

SECOND PERIOD
2. Rye—Ciolek (0:45).
3. Rye—J. Carter (11:00).
4. Dover—Dolan (14:10).

THIRD PERIOD
5. Dover — Din Fogarty (Sears) (12:05).
6. Rye—Peters (12:30).

PORTSMOUTH, N. H., FRIDAY EVENING, FEBRUARY 15, 1952

Seahawks Edge Wolfeboro, 4-3; Survive Rally

WOLFEBORO—After taking a 3-0 lead in the opening period and delivering a barrage of shots in the middle canto, the Rye Hockey club Seahawks had to resort to defensive play to gain a 4-3 victory over the strong home club.

Rye had dozens of shots off the Wolfeboro nets; but, none of them seemed to rip home as they caromed off the pads. Goalie Nelson was hit in the forehead by one of the shots and had to leave the game for medical attention. His place was taken by a defenseman and he continued to toss the shots to one side.

Effective poke-checking, a department in which Rye has not been too proficient this season, was the key to breaking up several Wolfeboro rushes. Harlan Carter led a number of rushes up the ice for the Seahawks after he had stolen the puck from the Wolfeboro line.

Rye had one goal, a shot by Guy Kelsey, disallowed and also had one allowed against them after a play definitely had been stopped before going over the line. The referee was not near the play and the goal judge did not reverse his decision.

The summary:

WOLFEBORO		RYE
Nelson	G	Meyer
Jutras	RD	H. Carter
Dunham	LD	W. Jenness
Melanson	C	J. Carter
Foss	LW	Ciolek
Clough	RW	Pearson

Wolfeboro spares: Grant, Githens, Davis, Buclea, Chamberlain and Graham.

Rye spares: Johnson, Remick, Drake and Kelsey.

The scoring:

FIRST PERIOD
1. Rye—Pearson (Ciolek).
2. Rye—Carter
3. Rye—Pearson (Carter).

SECOND PERIOD
No scoring.

THIRD PERIOD
4. Rye—Ciolek (Pearson).
5. Wolfeboro—Clough.
6. Wolfeboro—Jutras (Melanson).
7. Wolfeboro—Clough (Dunham).

Penalties: H. Carter (2) board check.

PORTSMOUTH, N. H., TUESDAY EVENING, MARCH 4, 1952

Rye, Nashua Tied In State League

STANDINGS OF THE TEAMS

	W	L	T	Pts.
Rye Seahawks	2	1	2	6
Nashua	2	1	2	6
Laconia	2	2	1	5
Dover	1	1	1	3
Wolfeboro	1	3	0	2

With the ice conditions varying from day to day, New Hampshire's "B" league hockey teams still are having a rough season.

Rye Seahawks and Nashua are in the lead in the state division with Laconia and Dover right behind.

The first four teams are expected to qualify for the playoffs which will be held at Lynn after March 1. The two finalists in the round-robin playoff will be invited to the New England "B" tournament which is scheduled for the North Shore arena March 24-25.

The New Hampshire teams had hoped to play at least 12 games during the winter months, eight of them to count toward the league standings and the third as an exhibition or one which might be the rubber match in case of a split in the home and home series.

PORTSMOUTH, N. H., THURSDAY EVENING, MARCH 20, 1952

Hockey Tourney Is Canceled; Stars at Lewiston

New Hampshire's amateur "B" hockey league tourney, slated to open in Wolfeboro last night, was canceled because of poor conditions at the upstate rink.

The Wolfeboro skaters have been unable to improve conditions at their rink following the heavy snowstorms of the past two weeks. Snow removal equipment and labor shortages have hurt the chances of the cleanup.

Nashua and Laconia have poor ice conditions and Rye has none.

* * *

THE TOURNAMENT was canceled and the teams from the four communities will meet at a later date in Lynn's North Shore Arena to seek the bid to the New England championship tourney.

It is possible that the teams may get together this week and select an all-star team to take part in the Class A senior tournament at Lewiston, Me., this weekend. The Berlin Maroons will not be competing in this tournament and the place may be taken by the "B" teams of the area.

The Berlin club drew the New Haven Sailors in the opening round of the tournament. New Haven has a strong club; but, the "B" All-Stars might be able to collect and aggregation which would put up a good battle.

PORTSMOUTH, N. H., MONDAY EVENING, MARCH 24, 1952

Seahawks Play Nashua For Class B Ice Crown

Rye Seahawks and Nashua will play off for the New Hampshire amateur league championship Saturday night at 10:30 o'clock in the Lynn Sports Arena.

The Seahawks made their way into the finals of the tournament by defeating the Wolfeboro sextet, 6-2, at Lynn last week.

Nashua, however, had an easier time. Laconia could not make arrangements to meet the Nashua hockey team so it had to lose its right to play for the title.

The Nashua and Rye clubs will be entered in the New England Class B tournament which is scheduled to get underway next week in the Lynn Arena. Play will be held on Tuesday, Thursday and Saturday and the pairings for these games will be announced later.

PORTSMOUTH, N. H., TUESDAY EVENING, MARCH 25, 1952

Rye Misses Shots, Nashua Wins

LYNN—In a game which saw the enemy goalie make 59 saves, the Rye Hockey club Seahawks lost to the Nashua Royals, 8-4, in a clash Saturday night at the North Shore Arena.

Rye trailed by five goals before it could find the nets. Even when the count was 5-2 in favor of the winners, the Rye club still was in the game playing every move carefully, but still unable to find the nets.

Rush after rush up and down the ice failed to materialize as Goalie Berube of Nashua kept the gate closed.

Rye, Nashua and possibly Laconia will take part in the New England Senior Class B tournament at the arena here tomorrow night. The starting time of the first game is 7 o'clock, but the schedule for the New Hampshire teams has not been released as yet.

The summary:

RYE		NASHUA
Weeks	lw	Dionne
J. Carter	c	Ravenelle
Burns	rw	Re Joyal
Johnson	ld	H. Noel
H. Carter	rd	W. Noel
Meyer	g	Berube

Rye spares: Drake, Bray, Kelsey, W. Jenness, I. Jenness. Nashua spares: Bernard, Powers, P. Joyal, Ray Joyal, Sletterberg, Connors, Nolan.

FIRST PERIOD

1. Nashua—Ravenelle (Plourde), 1:53.
2. Nashua—Rene Joyal (W. Noel), 9:05.

SECOND PERIOD

3. Nashua — N. Dionne (Ray Joyal), 2:43.
4. Nashua—Powers (Ray Joyal), 6:25.
5. Rene Joyal (Ray Joyal), 7:52.
6. Rye — Drake (I. Jenness), 13:31.
7. Rye—R. Burns, 15:06.

THIRD PERIOD

8. Nashua—Mahoney (Bernard), 4:42.
9. Nashua—Bernard (Powers), 6:40.
10. Nashua—Powers (Bernard), 14:51.
11. Rye — J. Carter (Byrns, Weeks), 17:24.
12. Rye—Weeks (Burns), 18:31.

Penalties: Bray, handling puck; Nolan, hooking; H. Carter, tripping 2.

PORTSMOUTH, N. H., WEDNESDAY EVENING, MARCH 26, 1952

Seahawks Outskate Laconia

Rye Seahawks Play Laconia

Rye Hockey club Seahawks will play Laconia at 8:30 tonight in the New England Class A tournament at the North Shore Arena in Lynn, Mass.

The Nashua Royals, conqueror of the Seahawks in the state playoff at Lynn Saturday, will meet the Weymouth Cubs in the third game of the night. The Nashua-Weymouth starting time is 9:30.

LYNN, Mass. — With Johnny Carter pulling the "Hat Trick" by scoring thrice in second and third period action, the Rye Seahawks collected a 4-3 victory over Laconia in the opening round of the New England AHA Class B tournament here last night in the North Shore Arena.

Laconia yanked its goalie from the net in the closing minute of play, but still could not score on the fighting Seahawks.

At one time in the third period, Rye was playing with three defensemen as two of the players sat out a penalty in the box. Johnson and Harlan Carter were out in that session.

Nashua defeated Weymouth, 11-7, in the second game last night and Lynnfield Knights defeated the Woburn skaters, 5-1, in the third quarterfinal game.

Nashua gets a bye into the finals and Rye plays Lynnfield Thursday night for the bid to get into the finals.

The summary:

Rye		Laconia
Angers	G	Meyer
J. Poire	LD	H. Carter
Shaw	RD	Johnson
F. Lamere	C	J. Carter
Brough	LW	Amory
R. Poire	RW	Nichols

Rye spares: Remick, W. Jenness and I. Jenness. Laconia spare: Levasseur, Fredette, Hickey, P. Lamere and Richardson.

First Period

1. Laconia—Levasseur (Hickey, Fredette), 3:40.
2. Laconia—T. Poire (F. Lamere), 5:38.
3. Rye—Remick (J. Carter), 8:42.

Second Period

4. Rye—J. Carter, 0.08.
5. Rye—J. Carter, 8:10.

Third Period

6. Rye—J. Carter, 0:55.
7. Laconia—J. Poire, 4:27.

Penalties: R. Poire, hooking; Hickey, interference; Hickey, handling puck; Johnson, charging; H. Carter, holding, and Levasseur, handling puck.

The Portsmouth Herald, Portsmouth, N. H.
Monday Evening, December 22, 1952

State Amateur Hockey League Set

Rye Seahawks Join Four Other Teams In Tourney Bid

"Dear Santa,

"Send us a little ice. . ."

Thus rang the plea of the members of the New Hampshire Amateur Hockey League and its five teams which will be playing for the bid to the New England amateur tournament two months hence.

The league will be composed of teams from Rye, Nashua, Laconia, Wolfeboro and possibly one Massachusetts entry, Amesbury.

Manager John Carter of the Rye Seahawks has been taking an active part in the organization of the loop and hopes the teams will get some ice on their outdoor rinks so they will be able to start the season early next month.

Plans now call for a four-game schedule with each of the teams. There cannot be any regular dates established because the teams will have to play when the ice is suitable. The teams will schedule their own games.

✿ ✿ ✿

Players in the Greater Portsmouth area interested in skating with Rye Seahawks have been invited to get in touch with Carter, who resides in North Hampton.

The Rye club has its rink on Atlantic Avenue in North Hampton and it is located at the intersection of Woodland Road. The players have been clearing hummocks off the rink preparatory to making the first layer of ice.

Several of the veteran players who may return with the Rye club this season, besides Manager Carter, are Harlan Carter, Flash Jenness, Homer Johnson. Goalie Pete Meyer, Frank Ciolek, Bill Lorenz, Bill Jenness and Phil Drake. Rye also will have several of the Dover stars who joined the club late last season.

All the teams need is the ice upon which they may cavort and fire the disc into the nets.

The Portsmouth Herald, Portsmouth, N. H.
Wednesday Evening, January 19, 1955

Seahawks Tied for Second In Valley Hockey Loop

RYE — The Rye Seahawks are tied for second place in the Merrimack Valley Hockey League while undefeated Amesbury Maples are riding the crest of a seven-game streak to hold the lead by eight points.

League play rounded the first quarter of the schedule last week.

Rye has six points and is tied with the Haverhill Ryans.

Games are being played at the Phillips Exeter Academy rink on Thursday nights starting at 7 p.m. and at the Pow-Wow rink in Amesbury on Sundays at 1:30 in the afternoon and 7:30 at night. Games postponed because of bad weather are played off as soon as possible.

There is no admission charge at any of the games because the players pay their share for the use of the ice.

The Rye roster includes Bob Lovett, Frank Ciolek, John Carter, Bernie Karjala, Leighton Remick, Harland Carter, Irving Jenness, Bill Jenness, Jack Hayes, Bud Loosemore, Dave Bunting, and Dave Meehan.

The senior standings:

	W	L	T	Pts.
Amesbury Maples	7	0	0	14
Haverhill Ryans	3	3	0	6
Rye Seahawks	3	4	0	6
Newburyport MV	1	4	1	3
Exeter K of C	1	5	1	3

The junior standings:

	W	L	T	Pts.
Amesbury Sacred H.	4	0	0	8
Newburyport Boscos	2	2	0	4
Bradford Shell	2	3	0	4
Bradford Badgers	2	3	0	4
Bannon Hockey Club	1	4	0	2

About the Author

Former Navy test pilot Bruce Valley has been an amateur hockey goaltender for almost six decades. A jazz musician and poet, he is chief executive of an aerospace corporation in Alexandria, Virginia, where he lives with his wife, Nancy. They have two children and six grandchildren, several of them hockey players. His poetry volume, *Rye Harbor and Other Poems of the Seacoast*, has been out of print for three decades.

"With *Seahawk*, the author rescues a great and moving hockey story from oblivion and, in the process, creates a world where sport and the lives of players are explored in exquisite detail with assured, writerly poise. A fine literary descendant of Jack Falla's "Home Ice" and Peter Gzowski's "The Game of Our Lives." Like any good hockey book, it teaches us more about the world than hockey itself." —**Dave Bidini**, Author of *Tropic of Hockey* and *The Best Game You Can Name*

"A compellingly intimate sports book that will hopefully become a movie, *Seahawk* has the breadth, depth, and power to be read for generations." —**Tom Clarie**, author of two parapsychology research handbooks, the award-winning Explorers educational game, and a forthcoming Egyptian history titled *A Lighthouse for Alexandria*.

"*Seahawk* is the true history of a small New Hampshire over-achieving town hockey team. We played the toughest big city teams in New England in the late 1940s and 1950s. And I was there from beginning to end." —**John "Jack" Hayes, Jr.**, Rye Seahawk 1946–1960

"This deeply moving and beautifully written memoir provides an authentic, warts-and-all look at New England amateur "town team" hockey in the years after WWII as seen through a young boy's eyes. Filled with insight, passion and honesty, *Seahawk* also traces one goaltender's amazing half century in net, and captures the three classic themes: man against man, man against nature, and man against himself. An absolute "must read" for avid hockey fans everywhere." —**Rosemary Clarie**, author of *Just Rye Harbor*.

"Bruce Valley describes hockey's thrills and he captures the gritty intimacy of small town sports. A terrific read for sports enthusiasts, sports historians and those fans who have always wondered what goes on behind the goalkeeper's mask." —**Steve Clarkson**, author of *Patriot's Reward*

SEP 2013

© Peter E. Randall